The School Leader's Guide to
Special Education

MARGARET J. MCLAUGHLIN

KRISTIN RUEDEL

A Joint Publication

Essentials for Principals is a registered trademark of the National Association of Elementary School Principals.

555 North Morton Street
Bloomington, IN 47404
800.733.6786 (toll free) / 812.336.7700
FAX: 812.336.7790

email: info@solution-tree.com
solution-tree.com

Visit **go.solution-tree.com/specialneeds** to download the reproducibles in this book.

Printed in the United States of America

16 15 14 13 12   1 2 3 4 5

Library of Congress Cataloging-in-Publication Data

McLaughlin, Margaret J.
 The school leader's guide to special education / Margaret J. McLaughlin, Kristin Ruedel. -- 3rd ed.
   p. cm. -- (Essentials for principals)
 Includes bibliographical references and index.
 ISBN 978-1-935542-81-0 (perfect bound : alk. paper) -- ISBN 978-1-935542-82-7 (library edition : alk. paper) 1. Special education--United States--Administration. 2. Children with disabilities--Education--United States. 3. School principals--United States. I. Ruedel, Kristin. II. Title.
 LC4019.15.M176 2012
 371.90973--dc23
                                   2012005767

Solution Tree

Jeffrey C. Jones, CEO
Edmund M. Ackerman, President

Solution Tree Press

President: Douglas M. Rife
Publisher: Robert D. Clouse
Vice President of Production: Gretchen Knapp
Managing Production Editor: Caroline Wise
Copy Editor: Tara Perkins
Proofreader: Elisabeth Abrams
Text Designer: Jenn Taylor
Cover Designer: Rian Anderson

ACKNOWLEDGMENTS

Solution Tree Press would like to thank the following reviewers:

Renee Ashley
Learning Specialist
Liberty Ridge Elementary
Bonney Lake, Washington

Joni Baldwin
Associate Professor, Department of Teacher
    Education
University of Dayton
Dayton, Ohio

David F. Bateman
Professor, Department of Educational
    Leadership and Special Education
Shippensburg University
Shippensburg, Pennsylvania

William Bursuck
Professor, Department of Specialized
    Education Services
University of North Carolina at Greensboro
Greensboro, North Carolina

Luann Domek
Principal
Lone Dell Elementary School
Arnold, Missouri

Suzanne Drawbaugh
School Psychologist
Lake Braddock Secondary School
Burke, Virginia

Sandra M. Keenan
Principal Research Analyst
American Institutes for Research
Washington, DC

Jennifer L. Stringfellow
Assistant Professor, Department of Special
    Education
Eastern Illinois University
Charleston, Illinois

Annmarie Urso
Assistant Professor, Ella Cline Shear School
    of Education
State University of New York at Geneseo
Geneseo, New York

Melanie White
Special Education Teacher
Pease Elementary School
Austin, Texas

Solution Tree Press wishes to acknowledge the contributions of the authors of previous editions of this book: Jean Patterson, Nancy Protheroe, and Cathy Boshamer.

Visit **go.solution-tree.com/specialneeds**
to download the reproducibles in this book.

TABLE OF CONTENTS

Reproducible pages are in italics.

ABOUT THE AUTHORS

Margaret J. McLaughlin is the Associate Dean for Research and Education and professor in the department of special education at the University of Maryland. She is the author of five books and numerous book chapters and articles on educational reform policy and students with disabilities. Dr. McLaughlin's research focuses on special education policy, including investigation of the impact of education reform on students with disabilities and special education programs. She also directs the doctoral program in special education policy leadership development as well as a doctoral program focused on the use of large-scale data to conduct policy research. Dr. McLaughlin is an expert not only in domestic special education policy and students with disabilities but also in international education policy. She has consulted in the United States and overseas to help develop programs and policies that would include students with disabilities in general education programs. Before coming to Maryland, she was the executive director of the Joseph P. Kennedy, Jr. Foundation. As a teacher, she taught children with emotional disturbance and learning disabilities.

Kristin Ruedel earned her doctorate in special education policy from the University of Maryland in 2008. In her dissertation research, she used the Early Childhood Longitudinal Study (ECLS) dataset to examine predictors of disproportionality in special education. Dr. Ruedel currently serves as the project coordinator for the special education doctoral program focused on the use of large-scale datasets at the University of Maryland, works as a consultant for PowerUp WHAT WORKS, and teaches as an adjunct faculty member for Washington State University. In addition to her domestic work, Dr. Ruedel has worked with several countries as an international consultant to improve the educational opportunities for children with disabilities. Dr. Ruedel has experience as an educational consultant, was a research scientist at the American Institutes for Research, and served as a Peace Corps volunteer teaching students with hearing impairments.

To book Margaret McLaughlin or Kristin Ruedel for professional development, contact pd@solution-tree.com.

The Principal's Role in the Special Education Process

Principals across the country are faced with many challenges associated with educating students with disabilities. Since the passing of the No Child Left Behind Act in 2001, principals have faced new requirements to include students with disabilities in the same academic standards, assessments, and accountability systems as all other students. Principals are also expected to understand and implement a range of new policies, including how to identify students with disabilities, how to ensure that they are fully included in the general education curriculum, and what to consider in disciplining them. To meet these and other new requirements and to ensure that students with disabilities are provided with high-quality educational opportunities, principals need an understanding of the legal foundations and entitlements for students with disabilities and their families as well as a solid understanding of what practices and processes constitute effective special education.

The Individuals With Disabilities Education Act (IDEA) is the primary disability law that guarantees the educational rights of students with disabilities from birth to age twenty-one. The law was first passed in 1975 as the Education for All Handicapped Children Act (Public Law 94-142) and has since been reauthorized and amended numerous times. In 1997, the name of the law was changed to the Individuals With Disabilities Education Act, which it retains today. IDEA not only defines the educational rights of students with disabilities to an individualized education program (IEP) at no cost to the parents but also outlines the responsibilities of the state and school district to ensure that each student with a disability is receiving a free appropriate education in the least restrictive environment. While some readers may be familiar with the term *individualized education plan*, we use *individualized education program* to be consistent with the current terminology used under IDEA and IDEA-related laws.

Under IDEA, special education is defined as individualized instruction and services that are designed to address the unique learning needs of each student with a disability and enable him or her to progress in the general education curriculum. Special education is not a place or a program; it is specialized instruction, accommodations, and supports that are tailored for each student with a disability. The nature of these supports, as well as the settings where instruction takes place, must be carefully designed based on a student's needs.

Studies on school leadership suggest that students with disabilities attending schools led by principals who provide administrative support for special education are more likely to progress in the general education curriculum and have enhanced outcomes (DiPaola & Walther-Thomas, 2003). Effective principals who clearly understand the needs of students with disabilities; the statutes, regulations, and requirements of IDEA and No Child Left Behind (NCLB); and the instructional challenges that educators who work with students with disabilities face are better prepared to provide building-level support and positively impact special education outcomes. These well-informed leaders can facilitate the development of appropriate student placements, the use of effective research-based practices, and the development of a school culture that promotes a sense of collegial support among general and special educators (DiPaola & Walther-Thomas, 2003).

Since 2001, responsibility for special education has dramatically shifted from the central office to the school. This means that the principal must provide the leadership and oversight for all aspects of educating students with disabilities and is essential to ensuring school-level compliance with the law. Yet only a few states include knowledge of exceptional children in their principal licensure requirements (Education Commission of the States, 2008). As a result, many principals are learning about special education law and the students it serves on the job. It is our hope that the information in this book will facilitate this learning process and help principals and school leaders meet the demands to improve the educational outcomes of students with disabilities.

In this book, we first describe the legal foundations and entitlements surrounding special education, provide information on the best-practice research for serving students with disabilities and other diverse learners, and provide strategies for implementing inclusive programs. The remaining chapters will address key issues related to the implementation of the law and how principals can work to facilitate effective implementation of educational programs that support all students in the building.

Chapter 1, Understanding the Basic Rights of Students With Disabilities, introduces key provisions of the Individuals With Disabilities Education Act, such as free appropriate public education (FAPE), least restrictive environment (LRE), related services, and the rights of students with disabilities and their parents as defined in the procedural safeguards of IDEA. Section 504 of the Rehabilitation Act, the Americans With Disabilities Act (ADA), and Title I of the No Child Left Behind Act are described.

Chapter 2, Determining Who Is Eligible for Special Education, explains how students are referred for evaluation for special education, the evaluation process, and how eligibility decisions are made and by whom. An early intervention model called response to intervention (RTI) is described as well.

IDEA requires an individualized education program for every student who is eligible to receive special education and related services. Chapter 3, Developing and Implementing an Individualized Education Program, provides readers with detailed information about the process of developing an IEP, its key components, and the role of the principal in the development and implementation process.

IDEA and NCLB define how students with disabilities are to be included in statewide assessment and accountability systems. In chapter 4, Assessing and Teaching Students With Disabilities, we discuss the requirements regarding assessment and provide information about accommodations and modifications. Barriers to developing an inclusive school are discussed, and promising approaches for improving student achievement are provided.

Chapter 5, Discipline and Positive Behavior Interventions and Supports, explains the processes, as defined under IDEA, for disciplining a student with disabilities. Terms such as *manifestation determination*, *functional behavioral assessment*, and *behavior intervention plan* are described, and suggestions to avoid discipline problems are offered.

Finally, in chapter 6, Encouraging Parental Involvement, we focus on parents and ways to involve them in the individualized education of their students. Ways for schools to engage parents and build effective relationships are suggested. The book ends with a list of online resources, a guide to significant changes that appear in IDEA 2004, and a glossary of terms used in special education.

CHAPTER 1

Understanding the Basic Rights of Students With Disabilities

The Individuals With Disabilities Education Act is the primary U.S. federal policy that defines which students are eligible for special education supports and services and protects students with disabilities against discrimination (see appendix B, beginning on page 71, for a summary of key legal provisions in IDEA 2004). This federal law guarantees all students, regardless of their disability, a free appropriate public education (commonly referred to as *FAPE*). To be eligible under IDEA, a student must first be determined to have a disability that is consistent with one or more of the categories specified in the law, and the disability must have an adverse effect on educational performance that necessitates specially designed instruction to meet the unique needs resulting from the disability. Only students who meet the eligibility requirements are entitled to FAPE.

Questions Principals Ask

- What are FAPE, LRE, and related services?
- What rights do students and their parents have?
- What is required under Title I of the Elementary and Secondary Education Act (ESEA)?
- How do Section 504 of the Rehabilitation Act and the Americans With Disabilities Act affect schools?

Visit http://nichcy.org/laws/idea for a wealth of information about IDEA, including summaries of requirements, statutes and regulations, and training materials.

Free Appropriate Public Education

A free appropriate public education includes specially designed instruction in addition to appropriate related services (for example, speech and language services, occupational therapy, technology, and so on) without cost to parents or students. The individualized education program defines what is considered appropriate for each student with a disability. To create an IEP, a team of individuals referred to as the IEP team (which includes the parents, selected school personnel, and, when appropriate, the student) meets to review the student's evaluation data and determine the appropriate services and instructional strategies that will support the student in the classroom (see chapter 3 for more information about developing an IEP and selecting members for the IEP team).

The IEP is a critically important legal document as well as the foundation for educating a student with a disability. The process for developing the IEP and who should be involved in developing the IEP are carefully prescribed in law as part of the guarantee of FAPE. The IEP represents a contract between the school system and the student's parents or guardians. We will discuss this important document in more detail in chapter 3.

What is considered FAPE for any given child is to be determined by the IEP team. However, defining what is considered appropriate has been subjected to a number of legal decisions. The U.S. Supreme Court case *Board of Education v. Rowley* (1982) ruled that schools are responsible for providing an individualized education to students eligible under the law. However, the court also stated that the law did not intend *appropriate* to mean maximizing the fullest potential of each child with a disability. The court further defined FAPE as an education that is delivered in compliance with the student's individualized education program and is "reasonably calculated to enable the child to receive educational benefits" (Board of Education v. Rowley, 1982).

Additional guidance on implementing IDEA's statutes and regulations is provided at http://idea.ed.gov by the Office of Special Education and Rehabilitative Services (OSERS) and the Office of Special Education Programs (OSEP) within the U.S. Department of Education.

Least Restrictive Environment

IDEA also requires that students with disabilities be educated in the least restrictive environment and with their nondisabled peers "to the maximum extent appropriate" (Assistance to States for the Education of Children With Disabilities, 2009). The 1997 and 2004 amendments to IDEA emphasize that IEP teams must first consider providing special education in the general education classroom and may only consider other settings if the student cannot receive an appropriate education even with special supports and services. For most students, the general education classroom is the appropriate setting. However, some children may require other settings, and the IDEA regulations require that school districts must be able to provide instruction in the following settings: general classrooms, special classrooms, special schools, home, and hospitals and institutions.

Where a child is educated is based on multiple factors such as academic achievement, progress in the general education curriculum, and teacher and parent input, and it is the responsibility of the IEP team to evaluate all the data and document why a student might receive special education outside the general classroom. According to OSEP's 29th Annual Report to Congress, during the 2004–2005 school year, 96 percent of students ages six through twenty-one served under Part B of IDEA were educated in general education classes for at least some part of the school day. More than half of all students ages six through twenty-one served under Part B of IDEA were educated for 80 percent or more of the school day in general education classes (U.S. Department of Education Office of Special Education and Rehabilitative Services, 2007).

Under IDEA, more restrictive placements can be considered appropriate when the safety of the student with a disability or of the other students in the school environment is threatened or when the student with a disability is so disruptive that the education of the other students is significantly impaired. In these instances, documentation of the student's behaviors to support the more restrictive placement is essential. Exactly what documentation might be required will depend on your local district's policies, but most likely the IEP will require that the team indicate why it has decided to remove a student from the general education classroom. For instance, the statement might include evidence about specific behaviors such as vocal outbursts or aggression that may require a smaller, more controlled environment for learning to occur. These decisions are to be reconsidered at least once a year, and there should be evidence in the IEP that the interventions and supports that the student might require have been attempted in a general classroom.

Related Services

Under IDEA 2004, *related services* are defined as services that enable an individual student with a disability to benefit from special education. They are different from special education, which is specially designed instruction. IDEA includes the following items in its definition of related services an individual student may need to benefit from special education:

- Transportation

- Speech and language services

- Physical therapy

- Occupational therapy

- Interpreting services

- Audiology services

- Psychological services

- School health services

- Technology

- Recreation

This list is not exhaustive. However, IDEA does exempt surgically implanted devices and medical services unless those services can be provided by a trained layperson, including a teacher, school nurse, paraprofessional, or similarly trained individual. Related services are determined by the IEP team and specified on the IEP document.

Procedural Protections for Parents and Students

To protect the rights of students with disabilities and ensure their parents or guardians are meaningfully included in all decisions related to the student's special education program, IDEA provides procedural due process requirements. These are formal procedures and processes that the school must follow and are usually referred to as *procedural safeguards* or sometimes as *parents' rights*. They are intended to protect against school decision making that may prevent a student with a disability from obtaining a free appropriate public education. IDEA sets the basic requirements, but each state—and often districts—must develop their own policies and procedures that may be more restrictive than the federal requirements. It is essential for principals to have a firm understanding of their state and district procedural safeguards to ensure that the school is upholding the rights of the students in their building and those students' parents. They must be sure to follow the specific procedures and timelines set by their districts pertaining to such things as parent notices, required signatures, and so on. These procedures, which may be regarded as burdensome paperwork, are actually legal entitlements guaranteed under the law. The district special education administrator should ensure that each principal has a document that states these policies and procedures in his or her school and should ensure that it is available to parents as needed. This individual is the key contact in matters pertaining to special education and should be consulted in case of any doubt about a procedure.

Under the procedural safeguards in IDEA, parents are entitled to the following due process rights:

- Written prior notice of any actions related to their child and special education

- Written material provided in the parents' native language unless it is clearly not feasible to do so

- Opportunity to examine all records relating to their child, including identification evaluation, placement, IEP development, disciplinary notices, progress reports, and reports from service providers

- Right to obtain an independent educational evaluation of their child

- Right to participate in and agree to all decisions regarding their child's identification, evaluation, educational placement, and the provision of free appropriate public education

- Opportunity to present complaints regarding any matter relating to the identification, evaluation, educational placement, or provision of free appropriate public education for their child. School districts must have procedures in place for parents to follow when filing a written due process complaint and include information on how to complete a hearing request form. According to IDEA regulations, the hearing request form must include the student's name and address, the name of the school the student attends, a description of the complaint, and recommendations for a resolution to the problem (Seltzer, 1998). A parent's due process hearing request must address alleged violations that occurred not more than two years before the date that the parent or school district knew or should have known about the issue leading to the request.

- Written prior notice when parents and the school disagree on a course of action. This notice must include—

    > a detailed description and explanation of the course of action recommended or refused

    > a description of the evaluation procedures used to inform the decision about the recommended or refused course of action

    > a description of alternative options considered by the IEP team and explanation of why those options were deemed inappropriate for the student with a disability

    > a procedural safeguards statement identifying the rights of the parent(s) of the student with a disability as defined in IDEA

    > organizations for parents to contact to learn more about their rights and the rights of their student

    > any additional information that was considered by the school regarding the course of action in dispute

- Opportunity for mediation. The outcomes of mediation are considered enforceable as a settlement agreement.

- Opportunity to request a resolution meeting prior to presenting a complaint through a due process petition. Resolution meetings are considered less adversarial than due process hearings.

Additionally, students have the right to a surrogate parent when parents are unknown or legally cannot participate. A surrogate parent cannot be employed by any agency educating or caring for the child, should possess the skills and knowledge needed to represent the student, and is selected in accordance with state law.

Due Process Under IDEA

Procedural safeguards are grounded in the due process clause of the U.S. Constitution. Only a very small number of disputes that arise between parents and schools end up with parents filing a due process complaint. However, in the event that a parent should ever file such a petition, it is unlikely that a principal would manage this situation. The principal should notify the district special education administrator to make certain that all timelines and procedures are followed. It is not uncommon for parents to prevail in a hearing because the school did not follow specified procedures and timelines. For this reason, it is very important that principals know the procedures and timelines required by their districts and that they ensure compliance with these requirements.

A due process complaint (also known as a due process request or due process petition) must allege that a violation occurred not more than two years before the date the parent or public agency knew or should have known about the alleged violation.

Information required in a due process complaint includes the following:

- Name of the child

- Address of the residence of the child

- Name of the school the child is attending

- A description of the nature of the problem of the child relating to the proposed or refused initiation or change, including facts relating to the problem

- A proposed resolution of the problem to the extent known and available to the party at the time (Assistance to States for the Education of Children With Disabilities, 2010e)

If the parents and school district are unable to resolve the issue through an alternative dispute resolution process within thirty days of filing the request for a hearing, a forty-five-day due process hearing timeline begins. This means that a due process hearing must be held and a final decision issued within forty-five calendar days of the end of a resolution period. Either the parents or the school district has the right to appeal a final due process decision to state superior or federal district court within ninety days of the decision.

Alternative Dispute Resolutions

IDEA includes provisions to help parties reach an agreement through mediation or a resolution meeting in hopes of avoiding a due process hearing. The 2004 amendments to IDEA added a resolution process that schools must adhere to after receipt of a due process complaint. Specifically, IDEA now states that within fifteen days of receiving a due process complaint, the school district is required to schedule a resolution meeting with the parents and selected IEP team members unless the parents and school district agree in writing to waive the meeting or agree to participate in mediation instead of a resolution meeting. School districts are not permitted to bring a lawyer to the resolution meeting unless the parents of the student with a disability bring a lawyer. It should be noted that while a resolution meeting is now required when a parent submits a due process complaint, if the complaint is initiated and filed by the school district, IDEA does not require a resolution meeting prior to a due process hearing.

The purpose of the resolution meeting is for the school and parents to have an opportunity to meet, discuss the complaint, and resolve the problem without having to resort to a due process hearing. IDEA explicitly states that participants in the resolution meeting must include IEP team members who have information about the due process complaint and who were selected, in agreement, by the parents and the school or school district. Once the meeting is scheduled, if the parents do not attend, then the school has the right to ask the hearing officer to dismiss the due process complaint.

IDEA also requires schools and school districts to develop and make available processes to provide mediation to parents as an alternative to a due process hearing. Mediation is voluntary and provided at no cost to the parents. Parents may opt for mediation instead of a resolution meeting if they prefer that the process be facilitated by an objective third-party individual. A mediator is assigned to each case by the state to guide effective communication between the parents and the school and assist them in the process of resolving the dispute by facilitating a mediation meeting. The state is required by IDEA to maintain a current list of qualified persons that can serve as mediators. Mediators must have expertise in IDEA's statutes and regulations as well as individualized instruction, special education, and related services.

The collaborative approach of mediation is intended to encourage parents and the school system to work together to seek solutions to the issues in the dispute. The purpose of mediation is to discuss the issues and explore the options in an attempt to resolve the dispute. The use of mediation reduces time and other resources spent in litigation. In both the resolution meeting and the mediation meeting, if a solution to the problem is agreed upon by the parents and the school, all participants are required to sign a legally binding document which states the problem and the agreed-upon solution.

However, participation in the mediation process is optional; parents have the right to refuse mediation and can opt to move directly to a due process hearing. Furthermore, principals cannot use mediation to stall or delay a parent's due process request. IDEA sets specific timelines governing the scheduling and decision making surrounding mediation to ensure that parents' concerns are addressed in a timely fashion. If the parent(s) agree to the process of mediation, a mediation conference must be scheduled within fifteen calendar days of receiving the due process complaint, and a resolution that the parents and school agree to must be signed within thirty days of receiving the due process complaint.

Expedited Due Process

Parents and school districts have the right to request an expedited due process hearing when the dispute results from a disciplinary action and concerns a student's placement or determination of manifestation. Either the parent or the school district can file the expedited due process complaint and request. Regardless of who brings the complaint, the school system is responsible for scheduling the due process hearing and ensuring that all expedited timelines are met. Once the expedited due process complaint is received, the school is responsible for convening a resolution meeting within seven days unless the parents and the school agree to waive the resolution meeting. If the dispute cannot be resolved in the resolution meeting, the expedited hearing must occur within twenty school days of the request, and an administrative law judge must issue a decision within ten school days after the hearing. Although the timeline is considerably shortened, IDEA mandates that the expedited hearing maintain the same requirements as stipulated for general due process hearings such as a right to counsel and presentation of evidence with the opportunity to cross examine. IDEA does give states the authority to develop and implement alternate timelines and rules for expedited due process complaints and hearings. Therefore, it is important to ensure that you are familiar with your state procedures as well as the requirements specified in IDEA. Generally, state guidelines can be located on your state's education website.

Students With Disabilities and No Child Left Behind

In addition to IDEA, there are specific requirements pertaining to students with disabilities in the No Child Left Behind Act. Together, NCLB and IDEA define how students with disabilities are to be assessed and how schools will be held accountable for their performance and educational improvement. NCLB also specifies that *all* students, including those with disabilities, are to access and be held accountable for achieving the same grade-level content standards as all other students in the building. The expectation that students with disabilities should be fully included in grade-level state standards is designed to eliminate some historical problems in special education, including lower expectations for student learning, isolated IEP goals, and special education instruction focused primarily on low-level skills (McLaughlin, 2009).

Both IDEA and NCLB policies require that all students with disabilities are included in statewide assessments and that their progress in achievement not only be reported as a separate subgroup but also be included in the schoolwide calculations. While IDEA and NCLB both demand that all students with disabilities be included in statewide assessments, the laws still recognize the importance of individualization, a cornerstone in special education, by providing several ways for students with disabilities to participate in the statewide assessments. A student's IEP is expected to reflect grade-level *content* standards, but certain students may be assessed against different *achievement* standards. There are five ways that a student with a disability may be assessed: (1) regular assessment without an accommodation, (2) regular assessment with accommodations, (3) alternate assessment based on grade-level achievement standards, (4) alternate assessment based on modified achievement standards, and (5) alternate assessment based on alternate achievement standards (see chapter 4 for more detailed information about accommodations and modifications of assessments).

Alternate achievement standards only apply to students with significant cognitive disabilities and are defined as "an expectation of performance that differs in complexity from a grade-level achievement standard" (U.S. Department of Education, 2005, p. 20). In addition to alternate achievement standards, states have the option of developing modified achievement standards for students whose disabilities are so severe that they are unable to achieve grade-level proficiency or progress in the same time frame as other students (McLaughlin, 2010). Only a very few states have developed modified achievement standards, and it is unlikely that these standards will be continued when NCLB is reauthorized. As of this writing, draft legislation for this reauthorization has been released.

Visit http://www2.ed.gov/policy/elsec/guid/states/index.html for more information on NCLB and students with disabilities.

Highly Qualified Special Education Teacher

Another provision in both NCLB and IDEA refers to highly qualified special education teachers. Under IDEA 2004, a highly qualified special education teacher is defined as someone holding full state certification and meeting the same requirements as general educators if he or she teaches core academic subject matter (such as English, reading or language arts, mathematics, science, foreign languages, civics and government, economics, art, or history and geography) at middle and high school levels. Teachers of students held to alternate achievement standards in middle and high school should be certified or qualified in "subject matter knowledge appropriate to the level of instruction being provided" ("Q and A," 2007).

These requirements have implications for where and from whom a student with a disability receives his or her instruction. Middle or secondary students with disabilities must receive instruction in the previously mentioned content areas from teachers—special or general education—who are considered qualified by their state to teach that content. The "generic" special education teacher cannot be the primary instructor in these areas. It can be very difficult to find a teacher who is qualified in certain content areas such as algebra, geometry, or the physical sciences *and* in teaching students with disabilities. This requirement has led to increased use of co-teaching and collaborative models (which we discuss in chapter 4) that enable teachers to share expertise and collectively determine how best to deliver the content to every student.

Defining a Highly Qualified Special Education Teacher

In general, to be considered a highly qualified special education teacher, IDEA requires the following (Assistance to States for the Education of Children With Disabilities, 2010b):

- Full state certification or licensure as a special education teacher

- No waiving of certification or licensure requirements on an emergency, temporary, or provisional basis

- A minimum of a bachelor's degree

However, there are different requirements for special education teachers who teach core academic subjects, alternative achievement standards, and multiple subjects. Please visit http://nichcy .org/schools-administrators/hqt for more information about the federal requirements for highly qualified special education teachers. For a list of additional resources that contain information on staff development and qualified personnel, see the section on qualified personnel in appendix A (page 68).

Visit **go.solution-tree.com/specialneeds** for links to the websites mentioned in this book.

Section 504 of the Rehabilitation Act and the Americans With Disabilities Act

In addition to IDEA, two civil rights laws that prohibit discrimination on the basis of an individual's disability include (1) Section 504 of the Rehabilitation Act and (2) the Americans With Disabilities Act. Any student with a documented disability is covered under Section 504, but not all of these students are eligible under IDEA.

Section 504

Section 504 protects both children and adults with disabilities from discrimination in institutions receiving federal funds. Under Section 504, administrators, teachers, school psychologists, and other school personnel are required to identify students with disabilities and provide these students with educational opportunities equal to the educational opportunities offered to their nondisabled peers. To qualify for protection under Section 504, an individual must be considered a handicapped person. Although the original definition of individuals protected under Section 504 was relatively narrow, the law was amended in 1974 to define a handicapped person as "any person who has a physical or mental impairment which substantially limits one or more of such person's major life activities, has a record of such an impairment, or is regarded as having such an impairment" (U.S. Department of Education, 1996).

The definition in Section 504 is much broader than the definitions of the disability categories provided under IDEA. Under this definition, students protected under Section 504 range from those with Tourette syndrome, asthma, AIDS, and diabetes to students with alcohol and drug problems. Thus, students who are eligible for IDEA services are also protected under Section 504 but not all students who are eligible for Section 504 services will be eligible to receive services under IDEA. Essentially, the definition of a disability in Section 504 encompasses all students who have an impairment that affects a major life activity.

The protection from discrimination provided through Section 504 also includes participation in extracurricular activities and architectural accessibility. Section 504 not only protects the rights of students at the preschool, elementary, secondary, and postsecondary levels in the classroom but also applies during school district programs such as afterschool care and summer programs (Yell, 2006). Persons who qualify under the protections of Section 504 may not be discriminated against in programs receiving federal assistance and are entitled to reasonable accommodations to facilitate their participation. A few examples of reasonable accommodations that schools may be responsible for providing include, but are not limited to, the following:

- Changes to the classroom environment such as seating arrangements, reduction of visual or auditory distraction, or use of study carrels or partitions

- Changes to the testing environment such as extending the amount of time to take the exam, providing the test orally, allowing for open-book testing, or allowing the student to dictate answers on a tape recorder

- Use of a student's behavior intervention plan

- Provision of textbooks and materials with enlarged print, highlighted textbooks, or books on tape

- Changes to homework and in-class assignments such as providing extra time to complete assigned work, allowing for written assignments to be delivered orally, or segmenting long assignments into discrete shorter tasks

Section 504 Key Provisions

In contrast to IDEA, there are no federal funds available under Section 504 to assist school districts and other institutions in meeting the requirements of the law.

Under Section 504, students with disabilities are entitled to:

- Protection from discrimination in elementary, secondary, and postsecondary schools
- School programs, structures, and activities that are physically accessible
- Facilities and services that are comparable to general education facilities and services in instances when the school operates a separate facility for students with disabilities

The Office for Civil Rights (OCR) in the U.S. Department of Education investigates complaints with a goal of reducing and eventually eliminating discrimination against students with disabilities. If a school district is found to be violating the requirements of Section 504, OCR will encourage the school district to enter into a corrective action agreement in order to address the problem. However, in the rare case that a school district refuses to comply with the requirements of Section 504, OCR has the right and responsibility to begin enforcement action whereby the case may be referred to the Department of Justice, or the OCR may terminate Department of Education financial assistance to the school.

The provisions of Section 504 are sometimes used as a basis for providing services for students who have learning difficulties but who do not have an IDEA-eligible disability. Some services provided under Section 504 include adaptation or modification of testing conditions such as providing exams in alternative locations, extending the allotted testing time, providing oral exams, and other reasonable accommodations (see chapter 4 for explanations of testing adaptations and modifications). However, Section 504 does not require schools to change the nature of their programs to accommodate individual students. And, as under IDEA, students who qualify for Section 504 protections may not be suspended, expelled, or otherwise punished for manifestations of their disability (see chapter 5 for an explanation of IDEA's discipline requirements).

Evaluation and Placement

In order to be protected under Section 504 and receive services, students must be evaluated and placed. Placement decisions are determined by a team of individuals (convened by the principal) who know the student, know how to interpret evaluation data, and know the variety of placement options available in the school or school district. Although the specific members of the team can vary by student, the team generally includes a general education classroom teacher and other school personnel with expertise that could be beneficial to helping the student such as a building nurse, the school psychologist, a social worker, and so on. As in IDEA, the team is required to use information from a variety of sources and base all placement decisions on the individual needs of the student. Once a student is identified as needing services under Section 504, the school should develop an individual plan to ensure appropriate accommodations are available to the student. Although a written document is not mandated by law, it is generally suggested as best practice to develop one and an individualized education program similar to that outlined in IDEA may be used as the Section 504 plan. The purpose of the 504 plan is to explicitly define accommodations or modifications needed by the student in order to successfully participate in the general education setting. Accommodations might include monitoring of blood sugar levels, provision of wheelchair ramps, a peanut-free lunch environment, or a tape recorder or keyboard for taking notes in the classroom setting. The 504 plan is a legally binding document that encourages consistency of accommodations and services provided to the student as well as accountability.

Procedural Safeguards

As Mitchell Yell (2006) explains, parents are entitled to a number of specific rights under Section 504, including the following:

- Right to be notified of procedural rights under Section 504

- Right to be notified when their child is referred, evaluated, and placed

- Right to notification when eligibility is determined

- Right to an evaluation that uses information from multiple sources and is conducted by knowledgeable persons

- Right of the student to have access to equivalent academic and non-academic services

- Right of the student to receive an appropriate education in the least restrictive setting, which includes accommodations, modifications, and related services

- Right to file grievance with the school district

- Right to an evaluation prior to making a significant programming or placement change

- Right to be informed of proposed actions affecting the program

- Right to examine all relevant records and request changes

- Right to receive information in the parents' native language or primary mode of communication

- Right to periodic reevaluations

- Right to an impartial hearing when a disagreement occurs

- Right to be represented by counsel in the hearing

- Right to appeal the hearing officer's decision (p. 137)

To ensure that the rights of parents are upheld, schools are responsible for establishing a system of due process procedures to protect the rights of parents of students with disabilities. Schools are encouraged, but not required, to use the procedural safeguards of IDEA as a guide for ensuring the procedural safeguards of Section 504 are met.

For more information on Section 504, including information on evaluation, placement, procedures, and discipline, visit the Council of Educators for Students With Disabilities website (www.504idea.org/Council_Of_Educators/Resources.html).

Americans With Disabilities Act

Congress enacted ADA in 1990 to protect against discrimination of individuals with disabilities. While many ADA provisions are similar to those defined in Section 504, ADA provides even broader antidiscrimination coverage by protecting individuals in both public and private sectors (Marshall & Patterson, 2002). Although most provisions of ADA are already covered under IDEA and Section 504, there are a few additional situations in which ADA affects school operations. For example, under ADA, school districts must ensure that all school events are physically accessible to students with disabilities. Therefore, school districts are required to provide a barrier-free school environment including access to specialty areas of the school such as auditoriums and athletic stadiums (La Morte, 2005). Although there are no direct funds attached to ADA, many federal agencies offer grants to support training and technical assistance on ADA requirements. Also, businesses, organizations, and schools that are working on removing architectural or transportation barriers could be eligible for a tax credit. Visit www.ada.gov/publicat.htm for more information about ADA regulations, organizations that provide technical assistance, and funding opportunities that are available to help support the implementation of ADA regulations.

The purpose of this chapter was to provide a general overview of IDEA and its key provisions and provide a basic structure for understanding special education policies, including not only IDEA but also Section 504 and the ADA. In the next chapter, we turn our focus to the detailed process of determining student eligibility for receiving special education and related services and to the role of the principal throughout the eligibility and evaluation process.

2

Determining Who Is Eligible for Special Education

Eligibility for special education is contingent on two criteria. First, a student must be determined to have one or more of the disabilities specified under IDEA, and second, that disability must adversely impact the student's educational performance.

Questions Principals Ask

- Who is eligible for services under IDEA?
- How is the decision made to evaluate a child?
- What information must be collected?
- What is RTI?

IDEA includes the following disability categories (Assistance to States for the Education of Children With Disabilities, 2010a):

- Intellectual disability

- Hearing impairment

- Deafness

- Speech or language impairment

- Visual impairment (including blindness)

- Serious emotional disturbance

- Orthopedic impairment

- Autism

- Traumatic brain injury

- Specific learning disability

- Other health impairment, including attention deficit disorder and Tourette syndrome

- Deaf-blindness

- Multiple disabilities

- Developmental delays (children ages three through nine)

The second criterion for services under IDEA 2004 states that the child's disability must have an adverse impact on educational performance. Not all children with physical or mental impairments satisfy IDEA's eligibility criteria. If the impairment does not present an adverse effect on educational performance, the student does not qualify for services under IDEA. Thus, the law does not assume that every student with a disability needs special education and related services. Rather, students who do not meet the adverse impact criteria of IDEA are covered under Section 504 and the ADA. For instance, a student may have a significant neuromuscular condition that impairs much of his mobility, including the ability to write. But such a student may be quite able to learn at the same rate and meet the same standards as his or her peers. Such a student may require accommodations ensured under Section 504, such as physical adaptations to allow for a motorized wheelchair, assistive technology such as speech-to-text software, or a scribe to help with writing tasks. Such accommodations might not require an IEP, but instead require an accommodation plan. There is no need for special education, but there is a need for access to the education that is provided to all other students.

There is no specific category for children with some types of disabilities such as chronic health problems or attention deficit hyperactivity disorders (ADHD). These children might qualify under one of the other categories or as other health impaired (OHI), but only if their condition substantially limits their ability to benefit from education and adversely affects their educational performance to the extent that they require special education and related services.

Identification and Evaluation of Students

There have been longstanding concerns about misidentification and the inappropriate placement of students, particularly minority students, in special education classrooms. There are also equally important concerns over the failure to identify students with potential disabilities. As a result, very specific regulations have been put in place that define the methods, processes, and timelines for evaluating students who are suspected of having a disability.

Schools are responsible for conducting comprehensive multidisciplinary evaluations of students considered for special education. The intent of the formal assessment and evaluation procedures outlined in the IDEA 2004 amendments is to ensure the following:

- Special education services are provided to those who really need them.

- Decisions to provide services are fair and defensible.

- Implementation of evaluation requirements across states and districts is consistent.

To ensure that the school is in compliance with the law and meeting the needs of all students in the building, it is essential that principals be well informed of the eligibility requirements of the law.

What Is Child Find?

Child Find is a system included as part of IDEA that requires that states and school systems be proactive in identifying children with disabilities by using specific procedures for screening and following up on suspected disabilities among all children residing in the state, including those children attending private schools. If a parent, teacher, or other school staff member suspects that a student might have a disability that is affecting learning, he or she should refer the student for an initial screening assessment to determine if the student may be eligible for services.

Must Parents Consent to Evaluation?

Parental consent for evaluation must be obtained before any individual evaluations are conducted. But parental refusal does not mean that the school district is absolved of its responsibility to determine if a student is eligible to receive special education services. In cases when parents refuse to give their consent, the principal may use counseling or mediation to encourage parental cooperation. In more difficult cases, due process proceedings may be initiated by a school system to obtain permission from a hearing officer. This step may be necessary to ensure that a student receives needed services and to protect the school from future liability for failing to provide that student with a free appropriate public education.

Who Is Involved in Conducting an Evaluation?

A team of school personnel, including an administrator, a special education teacher, a general education teacher, and a school psychologist, generally conducts the evaluation process. Specifically who constitutes a given team depends on the areas that have been identified as problems in the referral. The team is responsible for providing an individualized evaluation that specifically addresses the referral concerns, all aspects of the suspected disability, the characteristics of the student, and the student's learning and behavior patterns. IDEA includes detailed procedural requirements for the evaluation team to follow during the process of conducting an evaluation. Additionally, each district will have specific procedures for conducting initial evaluations. Principals need to be familiar with these procedures as well as the mandated timelines and ensure that they are followed correctly. Violations could result in a judge or hearing officer rendering the eligibility determination and IEP inappropriate and invalid.

The Components of an Evaluation

Eligibility evaluations must examine results from a variety of assessment tools and methods such as the following:

- Performance on statewide assessments

- Classroom observations conducted by the principal or specialized school personnel with expertise in the area(s) in which the student is experiencing difficulty

- Classroom-based tests and examples of student work on classroom assignments

- Parental information and input collected through interviews with the parent. Parents can provide a wealth of historical information relating to overall development of the student.

- Medical diagnoses when appropriate

- Psychological testing when appropriate

The goal of the evaluation is to assess physical, cognitive, behavioral, and developmental factors in the child in order to create a holistic picture of the student and their level of functioning both in the school environment and at home. The evaluation should be nondiscriminatory, individualized, and comprehensive. It should be administered in the student's native language to rule out limited English proficiency as the reason for the student's learning difficulties and must rule out lack of appropriate instruction in reading or math as a cause of the student's academic or behavioral difficulties.

After all data are collected, the evaluation team meets to review and discuss all available information. When interpreting evaluation data, the team must draw on information from a variety of sources, such as those noted in the preceding bulleted list. The team must ensure that all results and interpretations are clearly documented. Based on the data presented, the IEP team must determine eligibility. The final decision of eligibility reflects the opinion of the majority of the IEP team members and not just one member of the team. The final decision is then documented in written form. Any team members who do not agree with the final decision may attach a separate report detailing their opinions, concerns, and recommendations.

If a student is found to be eligible to receive special education and related services, these evaluation data will be used again by the members of the team of school personnel responsible for creating the student's individualized education program. Although it is often the case that many members from the evaluation team are also a part of the IEP team, it is not required that all members of the evaluation team also participate in the IEP team.

Reevaluation or Triennial Assessments

A student receiving special education and related services is to be reevaluated at least every three years unless the parent and the school agree that a reevaluation is unnecessary. These are referred to as *triennial assessments*. A student may be reevaluated more often if conditions warrant or if a teacher or parent requests a reevaluation. The purpose of a reevaluation is to determine if the student is still eligible to receive special education.

Schools are not required to conduct a reevaluation for students who are graduating with a regular diploma or who are aging out of eligibility unless the three-year reevaluation cycle falls during the year of graduation. However, school districts are now required under IDEA to provide the student with a summary of the student's academic or functional performance. The summary of performance (SOP) is written by the student's IEP team as an exit requirement, and IDEA mandates that the SOP include recommendations to help the student achieve his or her postsecondary goals. Additional information to include in the SOP is determined by state and local policies.

IDEA does not require that schools provide an SOP to students who exit secondary school with a GED credential or alternate diploma. In fact, these students remain eligible for a free appropriate public education under Part B of IDEA until they are twenty-one years of age or until they receive a regular diploma.

Response to Intervention

Response to intervention or *RTI* is a term for a process that is designed to prevent unnecessary referrals to special education. It is closely related to the prereferral teams that many schools have used to assist teachers with individual students experiencing learning or behavior problems. RTI can differ from other prereferral or problem-solving teams in the specific steps and even assessments and interventions that are expected to be implemented. RTI is also increasingly being used as a schoolwide early intervention model.

What Is Response to Intervention?

RTI is a carefully defined system of implementing high-quality, research-based interventions of increasing intensity to all students in general education and continuously monitoring student progress to determine if students are able to meet their academic and behavioral goals and if special education and additional related services are needed. RTI is implemented by general educators, with support or input from specialists, and it is not considered special education.

The basic RTI model is referred to as a *tiered intervention model*. The most common model of RTI follows this structure:

- **Tier 1** is instruction of all students in the general education classroom. At this foundational tier, student progress is carefully monitored using curriculum-based formative assessments. In addition, universal screenings (such as screening all kindergartners for letter-sound awareness) are implemented to determine which children are possibly at risk.

- **Tier 2** provides supplemental interventions, typically in small groups, in the areas in which a student has been identified as having a problem. Tier 2 interventions should be considered to be relatively short term—not more than six to eight weeks—during which a student's progress is carefully assessed.

- **Tier 3** is designed for students needing more individualized, focused, and longer-term interventions. Often these are one-on-one or small-group interventions. It should be noted that in some models, Tier 3 is provided by special education personnel and requires a comprehensive multidisciplinary evaluation. In other models, this tier is provided by general education personnel, and only students who fail to progress with this level of intervention are referred for special education evaluations.

Types of RTI Models

There are basically three types of RTI models: problem-solving, standard protocol, and hybrid models—

- **Problem-solving models** use student performance data to guide selection and implementation of interventions that will target the student's unique learning problems. Problem-solving models are generally created by a school-based team of individuals who have expertise in evaluating student data, identifying learning goals, selecting appropriate interventions that meet the targeted learning needs of the student, and assessing effectiveness of the interventions employed (VanDerHeyden, n.d.).

- **Standard protocol models** use a limited selection of specific interventions that have been carefully researched and that must be implemented according to strict procedures and timelines. Some of these are in the area of reading and have powerful effects on learners.

- **Hybrid models** use some of the components of each of the previous models: for example, a problem-solving model might use standard, prescribed assessment procedures to identify specific behavioral triggers or academic problems. This hybrid will have better effects than a problem-solving model that relies on verbal discussions and reports and ambiguous feedback to teachers.

RTI and Specific Learning Disabilities

As mentioned earlier in this chapter, there have been longstanding issues with misidentification of students. One of the issues has been the difficulty in defining and evaluating specific learning disabilities (SLD). The original definition was based on the notion of a discrepancy between the students' cognitive ability (such as an IQ score) and their classroom academic achievement. This meant that a student with an average or above average measured IQ had to demonstrate unexpectedly low achievement in one or more areas to be considered to have a specific learning disability.

There have been many concerns about the discrepancy definition and how it is measured since the passage of the Education for All Handicapped Children Act (Public Law 94-142) in 1975. There have always been concerns that many students would be identified as having a specific learning disability who were in reality not achieving due to other factors, such as poverty, language differences, and inadequate instruction. In fact, students with SLD have historically accounted for the largest group of students served in special education ("Fast Facts," n.d.a).

Critics of the discrepancy model have cited bias against students from diverse racial or ethnic backgrounds (who often tended to score lower on measures of IQ) as well as the "wait-to-fail" aspect of the definition that requires waiting to evaluate a student until there is a significant academic delay (typically two or more years) (Fletcher, Coulter, Reschly, & Vaughn, 2004; Fuchs, Mock, Morgan, & Young, 2003; Gersten & Dimino, 2006; Vaughn & Fuchs, 2003).

IDEA no longer requires that states use the discrepancy model for evaluating SLD. Districts may choose to use the response to intervention model as an alternative. What this means is that prior to recommending a special education evaluation, a student will have to receive several levels or tiers of carefully defined and increasingly specialized interventions with careful progress monitoring. Only those students who do not respond, meaning those whose achievement does not increase at each level, are referred for full special education evaluations.

Implementing RTI in the School

Implementing RTI requires strong schoolwide collaboration. It is important to have the right people involved, including master teachers, school psychologists, behavioral specialists, and any others whose expertise might be needed. Many schools now have RTI teams that are dedicated to the implementation of schoolwide RTI efforts. Who is included on these teams and the size of the teams depend on the culture of the district and school. Teams could include general education teachers, special education teachers, administrators, specialists such as speech and language teachers or teachers of English language learners, and so on. It should also be noted that the amount of professional development required cannot be underestimated.

Principals must first make sure that classroom teachers are using interventions that are research based and that they are continually assessing and reviewing the success of their instructional strategies and interventions to determine effectiveness. We will say more about these practices in chapter 4. Principals can support their teachers by providing the resources needed to efficiently and effectively implement new interventions in the classroom and by providing access to specialists or other teachers who can help identify new, increasingly intense interventions for students who are not progressing adequately.

Having a toolkit of assessments that teachers and other specialists can use to identify specific academic or behavioral areas in need of remediation or support is critical to the RTI implementation process. These assessments can include commercial tests and checklists but should also involve more informal curriculum-based assessments that can be reviewed and discussed by teachers to identify gaps in a student's knowledge. Sometimes, functional assessments are used to isolate specific interventions. Student performance is generally assessed before implementation of any interventions to develop a baseline for student performance. As targeted interventions are implemented, student performance is observed and retested to assess the impact of the intervention on student learning.

Being consistent in implementing an intervention is referred to as *fidelity,* and it is very critical to the success of the intervention. Classroom teachers must implement interventions exactly as specified over a sufficient time period, and they must continuously monitor student progress. It is also important to give an intervention time to work. Knowing when to try something else really depends on carefully monitoring a student's learning using simple curriculum-based assessments weekly or even more frequently. If a student is not showing any progress mastering a specific skill or changing a behavior, the intervention needs to be reconsidered. RTI can be a powerful model to address learning and behavioral difficulties among students and reduce misidentification of students for special education. When implementing any RTI model, principals must ensure that teachers do the following:

- Provide evidence-based general education practice.

- Carefully assess and isolate learning and behavioral problems.

- Monitor progress.

- Change the nature or intensity of the interventions when there is lack of progress.

Principals must be very careful that these interventions not have the effect of delaying the referral of a student eligible for special education services. A study conducted by the Office of Special Education Programs in the U.S. Department of Education found that some local education agencies were using RTI strategies to delay or deny a timely initial evaluation, which resulted in OSEP issuing a memorandum in 2011 emphasizing the importance of ensuring that prereferral procedures or practices do not result in delaying or denying identification (Musgrove, 2011).

Progress monitoring, a critical component of RTI, can be a helpful tool in ensuring identification for special education is not delayed or denied. Progress monitoring involves clearly defining what changes or improvements are expected as a result of interventions that are put in place and systematically assessing these using various types of measures daily or weekly. If a student is not responding (or, in other words, improving) after two weeks of an intervention, the RTI team should consider what might need to change. Perhaps the interventions are not being used or are not used as intended, or maybe new strategies are needed. However, if the team has assessment data and can also provide evidence that the interventions are being implemented, then a formal referral for evaluation should be considered.

To learn more about the components of RTI, including tips for monitoring interventions in the classroom, visit the National Center on Response to Intervention (NCRTI) website at www .rti4success.org, and visit the RTI Action Network website at www.rtinetwork.org/learn/what /approachesrti to learn more about RTI models and implementation.

The purpose of this chapter has been to outline the detailed process of determining student eligibility for special education and related services. Principals can use the information provided in this chapter to help ensure that they are appropriately identifying and serving students with special needs as required by law. In the next chapter, we explain in more detail the process of how to serve these students by creating and implementing individualized education programs.

3

Developing and Implementing an Individualized Education Program

An IEP is a written document that is developed according to specific procedures and timelines, sets forth specific educational goals for a student with a disability, and specifies exactly what special education and related services the school will provide to enable the student to meet those goals. The IEP, developed by a selected

Questions Principals Ask
- What is an IEP, and why is it important?
- What is a standards-based IEP?
- How must an IEP be developed?
- What is the role of the principal in IEP development and implementation?

team of school personnel, the parents of the student with a disability, and, when appropriate, the student with a disability (the IEP team), establishes what constitutes an appropriate education for each student with a disability and is a legal contract between the school and the student's family. This document also specifies where the student will receive special education (the least restrictive environment) as well as how he or she will participate in assessments and which accommodations will be provided.

The IEP is the foundation to ensure that each student with a disability receives a high-quality education program that includes individualized instruction and services that target their unique learning needs. Each IEP is a truly individualized document. The IEP process is designed to facilitate the involvement of teachers, parents, school administrators, related services personnel, and students (when appropriate) to create an educational plan that will directly address the student's strengths and needs (Küpper, 2000). The following list illustrates the multiple purposes and functions of the IEP process and resulting document.

As Bauer and Shea (1999) explain, an IEP:

- **Defines the educational program** that will enhance educational results for the student and facilitate successful progress in the general education curriculum

- **Is a communication vehicle** that enables parents and school personnel to jointly determine both the student's needs and the appropriate special education and related services

- **Provides parents and school professionals with the opportunity to resolve any differences** with respect to expectations or goals for the student

- **Provides documentation of resources** that have been committed to provide the student with the specified special education and related services

- **Is a management tool** to ensure that students are given the special education and related services they need

- **Is a monitoring document** used by authorized personnel from various government levels to determine whether students are actually receiving the free appropriate public education on which the parents and schools have agreed

- **Is an evaluation device** to measure the student's progress toward projected outcomes

What Must an IEP Include?

As noted in chapter 1, the IEP is the most important document in special education because it is the document that clearly defines the unique learning needs of a student. The IEP document is based on the results of evaluation and assessment data collected about the performance of the student with a disability. It is a legal document that defines the individualized education program for a student with a disability and describes how the school will provide the needed accommodations and modifications to facilitate the student's progress in the general education curriculum.

General Requirements

To help schools and professionals in the development of these documents, IDEA requires that each IEP document contain specific information, including the following (Assistance to States for the Education of Children With Disabilities, 2006b; Küpper, 2000):

- **A statement of the student's present levels of performance and individual needs, including both academic achievement and functional performance.** The IEP must specify how well the child is doing in school according to evaluation results, class assignments and other products, and observations made by teachers, parents, and other school personnel. Academic, behavioral, and extracurricular or social areas should be addressed. The IEP should specify how the disability affects involvement in the general curriculum and educational performance.

- **Annual, measurable goals that meet the student's educational needs that result from his or her disability.** These goals must enable the child to be involved in and progress in the general curriculum and meet any other educational needs resulting from his or her disability, should specify what the student can reasonably attain in a school year, and should be linked to the state general education curriculum standards. Goals may be academic, address social or behavioral needs, or relate to physical needs or other educational needs.

- **A description of how the student's progress in meeting annual goals will be measured and when reports of student progress will be provided to parents.** Parents of students with disabilities must be regularly informed of their child's progress toward his or her IEP goals. The progress reports must be provided at least as often as parents of students without disabilities are informed.

- **A statement of special education and related services that will be provided.** The IEP must list the special education and related services and supplementary aids and services to be provided to, or on behalf of, the child. The IEP must also indicate the date when services will begin as well as the location and how often the services will be provided.

- **A statement of all supplementary aids and services that will be provided to help the student meet his or her annual goals, be involved and progress in the general curriculum, and participate in extracurricular and other nonacademic activities.** These aids and services should be based on peer-reviewed research, whenever practical. This section of the IEP includes program modifications and accommodations or supports for school personnel that will be provided for the child.

- **Participation with children who are not disabled.** The IEP must explain the extent, if any, to which the child will not participate with children without disabilities in the regular class and in extracurricular and nonacademic activities.

- **A statement of all necessary accommodations to ensure the student is able to participate effectively in state- and districtwide assessments.** The IEP must state what accommodations or modifications in the administration of state or district achievement assessments are needed in order for the student to participate in the assessment.

- **If the student will not take the regular state- and districtwide assessments, a statement explaining why the student must take an alternate assessment.** If the student will not participate in a particular state or district assessment (or a part of the assessment), the IEP must state why the assessment is not appropriate and how the child will be assessed.

- **A statement of transition service needs.** Beginning at age sixteen (or younger if the IEP team determines appropriate), the IEP must include measurable postsecondary goals related to training, education, employment, and, where appropriate, independent living skills. The IEP should also specify the transition services (including courses, participation in a vocational education program, or other programs) required to help the student reach the postsecondary goals. With parental permission or student permission if the student is age eighteen or older, community agencies may be invited to attend IEP meetings to discuss transition.

- **Age of maturity.** Beginning at least a year before the student reaches majority under state law, the IEP must indicate that the student has been informed of any rights that will transfer to him or her upon reaching the age of maturity.

Numerous examples of IEP goals and forms can be viewed on the Family Village School website (www.familyvillage.wisc.edu/education/iepsamples.html).

Although IDEA does not require principals to be active participants throughout the development process of the IEP, it is critical that you are knowledgeable about and engaged in discussions about the procedures, timelines, and logistics. It is important for principals to ensure that the learning needs of students with disabilities are met and that teachers and other school personnel feel supported.

Setting

The IEP document also states where a student with a disability will receive his or her education. While IDEA does require school districts to make available a continuum of services and settings, it strongly supports placing students with disabilities in the general education classroom for as much of their educational day as possible. Further, the IEP must document the supplementary aids and services required for the student to receive an appropriate education as well as personnel that will be responsible for implementing the identified services and aids (Etscheidt & Bartlett, 1999).

IEP teams must begin with the general curriculum as the preferred course of study and the general classroom as the preferred setting. If participation in the general education classroom and curriculum cannot be accomplished with supplementary aids and services, then a different setting may be offered. If a student with a disability will not be educated in the general education classroom, the IEP team must support that decision by providing clear and detailed documentation that, even with various accommodations and modifications, the student is unable to progress in the general education curriculum. It is important to remember that regardless of where a student with a disability is educated, access to the general education curriculum must be provided by a highly qualified special educator. Special factors that the IEP team must consider in developing an IEP include:

- Appropriate strategies for a student whose behavior interferes with his or her learning and that of others, including positive behavior interventions and supports (PBIS) to address the student's behavior

- Language needs of a student with a disability who also has limited proficiency in English

- Instruction in Braille for a child who is blind or visually impaired, unless instruction in Braille is not appropriate

- Communication and language needs for children who are deaf or hearing impaired, including opportunities for direct communications with peers and professional personnel in the child's language and communication mode (for example, signing)

- Assistive technology devices and services, such as augmentative communication, special feeding equipment, computer technology, and so forth

Supplementary Aids and Services

Supplementary aids and services and program modifications and supports are intended to facilitate a student's inclusion in general education classrooms and other school settings, including extracurricular activities. They are also intended to help students meet their IEP goals.

According to Etscheidt and Bartlett (1999) the following should be considered when identifying supplementary aids and support services for IEPs:

- **Physical dimension.** Alternations to the physical classroom environment, such as room or seating arrangements or changes to classroom lighting, that support the student with a disability in the general education classroom

- **Instructional dimension.** Aids and services related to lesson planning and delivery, methodology, and assessment, including adaptations and modifications in lesson presentation, assignments, assessment, learning structures, organization and study skills, activities and curriculum, and assistive technology

- **Social-behavioral dimension.** Aids and services that would enhance appropriate behavior and reduce disruptive, interfering behaviors

- **Collaborative dimension.** Aids and services that pertain to personnel resources, such as one-on-one paraeducator assistance, co-teaching, resource room assistance, teacher consultation, and teacher training

- **Other dimensions.** Additional factors unique to the student not included in the previous dimensions. This "what else?" dimension facilitates identifying other aids and services that might be appropriate.

Developing IEP Goals

The IEP must state the individual educational goals for a student and the program modifications or supports that will be provided. The goals and supports must be related to how the student will be involved and progress in the general curriculum.

Standards-Based Goals

In the past, IEP goals and objectives focused on identifying skill deficits and strategies to alleviate those deficits. Today, IEP teams are expected to develop IEPs that will enable students with disabilities to learn the same content as other students and to show that they are achieving standards. As a result, IEP teams are now using state grade-level content standards to drive the IEP planning process. Most often, teams select state standards as IEP goals and then identify strategies for helping the student meet these goals. Some key questions for the IEP team to consider when developing a standards-based IEP are:

- What are the learning goals and objectives that general education students are expected to accomplish (usually based on the state and district standards) during the time frame stipulated on the IEP? All areas of instruction (such as reading, mathematics, science, social studies, physical education, art, and so on) should be included in this analysis.

- What is the student's present level of performance and individual needs in each of these content areas as compared to the expected goals and objectives required of students who do not receive special education and related services?

- How is the student's disability impacting his or her educational performance?

- What special education supports and accommodations could be implemented to improve the student's educational performance?

Additionally, for IEP teams to develop meaningful standards-based IEPs, three things are necessary:

1. The team must include individuals who deeply understand the core grade-level content and achievement standards.

2. The team must have access to curriculum-based assessment information that informs precisely which knowledge, skills, and concepts the student needs to have supported.

3. The team needs sufficient opportunity to discuss the curriculum expectations and student assessment data in order to develop a comprehensive program of special education services and supports.

IEPs require flexibility and options. They should never be developed based on what a school has or is willing to provide, but on how best the student can be supported. The IEP team has an obligation and should be encouraged to develop a program that is reasonably calculated—and defensible—that will enable the student to achieve the goals set by the team. (For detailed information on developing IEP goals, please refer to *Accessing the General Curriculum: Including Students With Disabilities in Standards-Based Reform* [2nd edition] by Nolet and McLaughlin [2005].)

Sometimes, the services or supports needed are not readily available in a school. For example, the IEP team may want some assistive technology that is not available. In which case, the principal has an obligation to contact the director of special education to see how to obtain such equipment. Another example of when a principal needs to provide leadership is if the IEP team determines that a student may need more intensive therapy or specialized instruction than can be provided within the existing staff resources. For instance, a school may have the services of a specialist, such as a speech and language therapist, physical therapist, or psychologist for only a certain number of hours during a week, but a student may require more time. In this case, the principal should be supportive of the team's decision and advocate for the team. However, the principal should also encourage teachers to think creatively about how to meet a student's needs within existing resources. First, the team needs to think about how some of the specially designed instruction might be provided by general education teachers or paraprofessionals with training and support from the specialist. Cross-age peer and adult tutors can also be trained in specific strategies that they might be able to use for focused, short-term intensive remedial work.

Who Is Required to Be Part of the IEP Team?

Writing, designing, and implementing an effective IEP requires teamwork. A team of professionals who know the student in addition to the student's parents and the student him- or herself (when appropriate) are responsible for designing and writing the IEP. According to federal regulations under IDEA, the IEP team must consist of the following people (Assistance to States for the Education of Children With Disabilities, 2006a):

- The parent(s) of the student with a disability

- A minimum of one regular education teacher if the student is or will be in the general education classroom

- A special education teacher or special education service provider

- A school administrator with expertise in individualized instruction as well as the general education curriculum and who is aware of available resources within the district

- An individual with experience in interpreting evaluation results

- A community service representative for students whose IEPs will include postsecondary transition goals

- The student, when appropriate

Certain IEP team members may be excused from a meeting if that member's subject area is not being discussed or if the member provides a written report to all other IEP team members prior to the meeting. A parent must agree in writing before the meeting to excuse a required IEP team member from the meeting. Parents and schools can also mutually agree upon alternative means (such as conference calls or video conferences) for participating in IEP meetings when team members are unable to attend in person.

Sometimes, as Küpper (2000) notes, "an IEP team member may fill more than one of the team positions if properly qualified and designated. For example, the school system representative may also be the person who can interpret the child's evaluation results." Also, although not required, it is considered best practice to include appropriate related services personnel (such as a reading specialist, speech-language pathologist, occupational therapist, physical therapist, psychologist, school nurse, and so on).

Parent Participation in the IEP Process

The parents of a child with a disability are expected to be involved in determining whether their child is eligible for services and in developing the IEP. Requirements for parental participation in the development, revision, and implementation of the IEP are outlined in IDEA as follows:

> The parents of a child with a disability are expected to be equal participants along with school personnel, in developing, reviewing, and revising the IEP for their child. This is an active role in which the parents (1) provide critical information regarding the strengths of their child and express their concerns for enhancing the education of their child; (2) participate in discussions about the child's need for special education and related services and supplementary aids and services; and (3) join with the other participants in deciding how the child will be involved and progress in the general curriculum and participate in State and district-wide assessments, and what services the agency will provide to the child and in what setting. (Assistance to States for the Education of Children With Disabilities, 2002)

To comply with the law and to enlist parents in a partnership to provide a quality education for children with disabilities, it is important for the principal, teachers, and support personnel to work closely with these parents. Finding out how parents feel about current efforts to involve them might be an important first step for many schools. Parents and teachers should be encouraged to discuss any issues or concerns as well as share thoughts on how best to support the student *prior* to the IEP meeting.

It is also helpful for parents and teachers to talk with the student, when possible, about his or her feelings or opinions. Parents and teachers should make lists of strengths and weaknesses, including what they believe should be key goals for the school year. Coming to the IEP meeting prepared will improve the process for everyone.

The Role of the Principal in the IEP Process

The IEP does not require that the principal attend all IEP meetings, but there are several other areas in which principal leadership is critical. Effective principals must ensure that:

- IEP teams have sufficient time to fulfill their responsibilities

- The IEP team has the teachers and other specialists required to develop each individual student's IEP

- Parents are notified, encouraged, and supported to participate

- Services and supports that an IEP team considers important will be made available

- IEPs are accessible to everyone who will implement the program (such as general education teachers, special education teachers, and appropriate related services providers)

Just as principals set the tone for the school environment at large, they also set the tone for IEP teams. Principals should communicate to all IEP team members their support of the process as well as understand the legal and educational importance of an IEP. They must also establish and convey to IEP teams their expectations regarding the achievement of students with disabilities. While there are many ways that a principal can show support for students with disabilities, supporting IEP teams is one of the most important.

Implementing the IEP

Once the IEP is completed and the parents have given their written approval for services to be provided, everyone who will be implementing the IEP must have access to the document, including, when appropriate, the student. Specifically, each teacher and provider of services must have access to the child's IEP and must be informed of the following (Assistance to States for the Education of Children With Disabilities, 2010d):

- His or her specific responsibilities related to implementing all aspects of the IEP

- The specific accommodations, modifications, and supports that must be provided to the student

- How student progress will be measured and reported

The importance of developing and implementing an IEP that targets each student's unique learning needs and enables the student to progress and meet their education goals cannot be overstated. The IEP process ensures that students with disabilities are receiving the individualized special education instruction and services that are intended under the IDEA. Figure 3.1 provides a summary of the ten steps that compose the special education process as it relates to the IEP.

Step 1: Student is identified. Schoolwide screening activities, a referral from a teacher or other school professional, or a request from a parent identifies a student as possibly needing special education and related services. If the student's suspected impairment is a specific learning disability, scientifically proven research-based interventions designed to increase the student's rate of learning may be implemented in the general education classroom prior to a referral for evaluation to determine eligibility for special education and related services.

Step 2: Student is evaluated. As an article on the National Dissemination Center for Children With Disabilities website states, "The initial evaluation must be conducted within 60 days of receiving parental consent for the evaluation—or if the State establishes its own timeframe for conducting an initial evaluation, within that timeframe" ("Evaluating Children for Disability," 2010). Parents must provide consent before a school district can begin the evaluation process. The purpose of the evaluation is to establish if the student is eligible for special education and related services. The student must be assessed in all areas related to his or her suspected disability, and the evaluation must include multiple forms of data (evaluation results cannot rest on the results from only one test). All assessments and evaluation materials used to assess the student academically, developmentally, and functionally must be provided and administered in the student's native language. If the school uses the response to intervention model, the student's progress-monitoring data are an important part of

Figure 3.1: The special education process under IDEA.   continued →

the evaluation. In addition to the evaluation conducted by the school, parents have the right to have their student evaluated by a third party at no cost to the parent.

Step 3: Eligibility is determined. Selected school personnel (generally including the school psychologist, special education teacher, special education service providers, and administrators with expertise in interpreting evaluation results and special education) and the parents examine all evaluation results to determine whether the student is a child with a disability as defined by IDEA and whether this disability has an adverse effect on learning. The resulting decision from the meeting is referred to as the *eligibility decision*. Students may not be classified as having a disability if low academic achievement is found to be due to inappropriate instruction in reading or math or limited English proficiency. Under the procedural safeguards provided in IDEA, parents have the right to file a due process complaint if they do not agree with the eligibility decision.

Step 4: Student is found eligible for services, and IEP team members are determined. Once a student has been determined eligible to receive special education and related services as defined by the classification definitions under IDEA, the school is responsible for selecting a team of individuals that will serve on the IEP team for the student. At a minimum, the IEP team should consist of at least one general education teacher, a special education teacher, a school administrator, specialized school personnel with expertise in the areas needed to support the students' learning needs, and school personnel who are able to interpret evaluation results. In addition to school personnel, the parent(s) of the student with a disability should be a member of the IEP team as well as the student when appropriate.

Step 5: IEP meeting is scheduled. The school is now responsible for scheduling and facilitating an initial IEP meeting. A selected member of the IEP team will contact the parents to inform them of the purpose of the initial IEP meeting, tell them who is on the IEP team and will be in attendance at the meeting, and provide logistic information such as the time and date of the meeting. The meeting should be scheduled during a time that is convenient to the parents, and if the parents are unable to attend the meeting in person, the school must provide alternative means for the parent to participate (for example, conference call, video conference, and so on).

Step 6: IEP meeting is held, and IEP is written. The primary purpose of the initial IEP meeting is to develop an individualized education program for the student by setting academic, functional, and behavioral goals that are appropriate for the unique learning needs of the student. Once the IEP

goals and instructional plan have been developed, the school district must obtain written consent from the parent to implement the IEP and begin special education and related services. Parents who do not agree with the decisions made during the initial IEP meeting have the right to refuse consent and file a due process complaint.

Step 7: Services are provided. Once the parent has given consent to begin implementation of special education and related services, the school is responsible for providing instruction, related services, supports, accommodations, and modifications in accordance with the IEP document. Also, a copy of the legally binding IEP is provided to all teachers and service providers that will be working with the student as well as the parents of the student.

Step 8: Progress is measured and reported to parents. Methods for assessing student progress are defined in the IEP. Teachers are responsible for the ongoing assessment of the student's progress in meeting their intended IEP goals. The school is responsible for providing parents with student progress reports regularly throughout the year. Parents must be provided with updates on student progress as often or more frequently than parents of nondisabled students receive information about their students' progress.

Step 9: IEP is reviewed. The IEP is not a static document. Rather, it is a document that changes and grows with the student as the student meets his or her IEP goals and continues to progress through his or her education. Therefore, the IEP team must review the student's IEP at least once a year (more often at the request of the parents or school). When appropriate, new IEP goals are developed and, when necessary, instructional supports, accommodations, modifications, and instructional interventions are changed. Parents must be informed of IEP review meetings and have the right to offer recommendations for changes in the IEP goals and the student's placement.

Step 10: Student is reevaluated. At least every three years and not more often than once a year (unless the parent and the public agency agree otherwise), the student must be reevaluated to determine if the student still qualifies to receive special education and related services (Assistance to States for the Education of Children With Disabilities, 2010c). This evaluation is often called a *triennial evaluation*.

Source: Adapted from Küpper, 2000

Figure 3.1: The special education process under IDEA.

As discussed throughout this chapter, the IEP is an essential process and document that ensures students who have been identified as eligible to receive special education and related services will receive an education that is individualized and targeted to support their unique learning needs. Principals can be instrumental throughout the process by providing support and creating a shared vision for providing quality individualized instruction to students with disabilities in their schools. The following chapter will turn our attention to assessing students with disabilities as required under IDEA and NCLB.

4

Assessing and Teaching Students With Disabilities

Changes made to IDEA in 1997 and again in 2004 have attempted to align many of the requirements of that law with those of Title I of the No Child Left Behind Act (formally the Elementary and Secondary Education Act or ESEA). As we noted in chapter 1, both NCLB and IDEA emphasize the importance of improving academic achievement and the educational outcomes of all students, including students with disabilities. Together, these laws require that students with disabilities participate, with

Questions Principals Ask

- What are the legal requirements regarding assessing students with disabilities?
- What are accommodations, and how are they different from modifications?
- What are some keys—and some barriers—to developing effective and inclusive special education services?
- What are some promising approaches to achieving high levels of learning for children with disabilities?

appropriate accommodations, in all local and state assessments and that the results of these assessments be used to hold schools and school districts accountable for student achievement.

Accommodations and Modifications

Only a very small percentage of students with disabilities will be assessed using alternate (or modified) achievement standards. The majority of students with disabilities will take the regular assessments, and many will take the assessments with accommodations. It should be noted that each state has an approved list of accommodations that may be used during the state assessment. However, determining which accommodations might be appropriate for each student is an important decision and requires the IEP team to distinguish between accommodations and modifications.

An accommodation does not change the academic content or the achievement standard, and the student is expected to learn and work toward the same state-determined standards as students without disabilities. An accommodation provides the student with a disability with the supports intended to offset the impact of the disability so that the student is able to effectively access the content standards and provide a valid indication of what they have learned on an assessment. IDEA offers the following types of assessment accommodations:

- Presentation (e.g., repeat directions, read aloud, large print, Braille, etc.)

- Equipment and material (e.g., calculator, amplification equipment, manipulatives, etc.)

- Response (e.g., mark answers in book, scribe records response, point, etc.)

- Setting (e.g., study carrel, student's home, separate room, etc.)

- Timing/Scheduling (e.g., extended time, frequent breaks, etc.) (National Center on Educational Outcomes, 2011)

The IEP team must be sure that accommodations selected are appropriate for a specific student with a disability and that the student has access to accommodations during instruction. Not every accommodation that a student accesses in the instructional environment may be permitted during an assessment. Knowing the impact of the accommodation on a student's performance is necessary to make these decisions.

A modification differs from an accommodation in that it is intended to change either the content or the performance expectation. The key difference between a modification and an accommodation is the effect that it has on what a student learns or is expected to demonstrate on an assessment. For example, reducing the number of assignments or amount of reading material a student might cover in a grading period might be either an accommodation or a modification depending on whether the student is still covering the core standards and expected to meet the same level of achievement. In other words, if the student struggles with reading but is progressing in the general education curriculum and is expected to meet age-appropriate standards, then a reduction in the amount of reading material would be an example of an accommodation. In contrast, if the student is not expected to meet grade-level standards and has IEP goals that represent alternate achievement standards, then it is likely that the reduction in reading material requires that the text is rewritten at the appropriate reading level and, therefore, would be considered a modification. However, it is very important that teachers who deeply understand the curriculum and the expectations regarding what a student is expected to learn and demonstrate participate in decisions regarding accommodations versus modifications. Some primary guidelines to follow when determining whether an accommodation or modification is more appropriate are as follows:

- Make assessment and accommodation decisions on a student-by-student basis.

- Maintain a close link between instructional and assessment accommodations for each student.

- Make certain that individuals who deeply understand the specific grade-level curriculum expectations determine what constitutes an accommodation versus a modification.

- Keep abreast of emerging research on assessment and instructional accommodations, and state accommodation policies.

- Collect data regarding the number and types of accommodations being used, and review the data to ensure that IEP teams are individualizing and teachers are able to implement the accommodations.

Assessments

Historically, students with disabilities did not have to participate in state or local assessments, and often, when they were assessed, usually with accommodations, their scores were not included in reports or used for accountability. Schools were not held accountable for demonstrating that students with disabilities were progressing in the general education curriculum. A student's special education program was often separated from what was going on in the general education curriculum, and IEPs set isolated and individual learning goals that too often focused on low-level skills. Since the passing of the NCLB Act of 2001 and the reauthorization of IDEA in 2004, students with disabilities must now be included in the accountability systems. Their scores can no longer be thrown out and are not only reflected in the school- and districtwide data at large but are also separated for analysis as a subgroup. Schools are now responsible for ensuring that the subgroup of students with disabilities is progressing toward the goal of all students passing statewide assessments.

Following are some key questions and information that IEP teams should consider when determining the appropriate assessment for each student:

- **Which students will require assessment accommodations, and which accommodations are approved or allowed on the various assessments?** State accommodation policies differ both across states and across assessments, and IEP teams need to distinguish between accommodations that a student may require in instruction and instructional assessments to successfully participate in the classroom and progress in their learning versus those permitted on the high-stakes assessments. Accommodations must be clearly specified in the IEP, and the student must have use of the accommodation in instruction if it will be used during assessment.

- **Which students will take alternate assessments?** An alternate assessment may be based on alternate, modified, or grade-level regular achievement standards. Alternate assessments based on alternate achievement standards are to be available to students with the most significant cognitive disabilities and are grounded in grade-level content, and individualized in their depth, breadth, and complexity in order to meet the specific needs of the student. A few states have developed alternate assessments based on modified achievement standards. Modified achievement standards are only appropriate for a very small percentage of students with disabilities and are intended for those who are learning grade-level content that is included on the general assessment but, because of their disabilities, may need more time to learn the content being assessed. Alternate assessments based on modified achievement standards are designed to measure student proficiency of grade-level content and are less difficult than general education grade-level achievement standards ("Alternate Assessments for Students With Disabilities," 2011).

Creating Effective and Inclusive Special Education

Knowing what works best and deciding which approaches and strategies to use for students with disabilities can often be a challenge. There are a number of options to consider when deciding how to develop successful inclusive classrooms.

Inclusive Education

In the past, it was common to have students with disabilities taken out of general education classrooms and sent to resource rooms or placed in special classes where they received instruction that was totally separate from what was going on in general education classrooms and the general education curriculum. Too often, instruction in these settings either focused on discrete skills that were only loosely connected to classroom curricula or served as tutoring sessions that provided students with help completing various classroom assignments. Not only did the student miss classroom instruction, but the general classroom teacher often did not feel responsible for adapting instruction or otherwise supporting students with disabilities, as they operated under the assumption that the special education teacher would fix the problem. Further, when special education teachers have large caseloads, they not only cannot provide individualized education, they also cannot follow up with students or collaborate and consult with the general education classroom teachers.

Today, the majority of students with disabilities are being educated in general education classrooms for 80 percent or more of their school day ("Fast Facts," n.d.b). According to research conducted by Walther-Thomas et al. (2000), collaborative schools tend to be more inclusive schools—these are schools that build on the concepts of teamwork and communication with the goal of providing a high-quality educational learning environment and supporting all students in the school, including students with disabilities and other students at risk.

Collaborative schools are grounded in building relationships between school personnel, families, the community, and students that foster communication and encourage working together toward a shared vision of providing quality education to all the students in the building. Principals leading collaborative schools are generally effective in building positive relationships and increasing the social capital of their school. Building these collaborative relationships is important to the success of special education efforts. As trust and communication increase and knowledge and skills are shared among professionals and parents, the individuals work more as a team and all participants benefit (DiPaola & Walther-Thomas, 2003). In truly inclusive and collaborative schools, neither children nor teachers are isolated by their roles or where they are educated. Students with disabilities are not viewed as the sole responsibility of special education personnel, and there is a sense of collective responsibility among general and special education teachers, paraeducators, and other staff.

Principals are key in building collaboration and teamwork among general and special educators as well as other specialists and in supporting the flexibility in schedules that enables that teamwork and ensures that every student is respected, valued, and learning.

Effective Instruction and Practices

To effectively provide students with disabilities the same opportunities as all other students to progress toward and achieve state standards, it is important to understand some of the more common and effective practices that support that achievement. With the dual emphasis on providing every student with instruction focused on standards and on having inclusive classrooms, attention is increasingly being given to providing instruction in general education classrooms that meets the needs of many students with disabilities as well as other low-achieving students. Many of the interventions and strategies that have been proven to be effective with students with disabilities also are effective with other low achievers or struggling learners. Similarly, general education teachers can draw upon their knowledge regarding teaching and learning to make adaptations to design unique learning experiences for students.

> Visit the Co-Teaching Connection website at www.marilynfriend.com for more information and valuable resources for administrators, teachers, and parents on co-teaching.

Collaborative or Co-Teaching

Creating a partnership through co-teaching can be an important strategy for meeting the diverse learning needs of all students in the classroom. Collaborative or co-teaching refers to an educational approach in which general and special educators work together to jointly teach academically and behaviorally heterogeneous groups of students. The collaborative teaching approach maximizes the specific and unique skills that general and special educators bring to the school. For example, most general educators are knowledgeable about curriculum and curricular sequencing, especially in traditional academic content areas. They are also skilled and experienced in managing large groups. Special educators have typically developed expertise in targeting areas of difficulty within a curriculum and analyzing and adapting instructional materials and strategies. These skills are now more in demand in the general education classroom as teachers are faced with a more diverse student population. Special educators also have expertise in developing IEPs and behavior management techniques. Working together, the two professionals can bring an impressive combination of skills to the classroom (Bauwens, Hourcade, & Friend, 1989).

Collaborative teaching models are designed to help students with learning or behavior problems function more successfully in general education classrooms by providing structured support to the student. These models also increase the professional interaction among general and special education classroom teachers and increase the possibility that other struggling learners in the classroom can receive assistance (Walther-Thomas, Bryant, & Land, 1996). However, collaborative teaching cannot be effective if classes are overloaded with students who require special attention. Nor can the models work if teachers have not had adequate time to learn the various approaches to co-teaching or if they do not have time to plan together. Principals can support effective implementation of co-teaching strategies by providing teachers with essential planning time and professional development opportunities.

Providing Options for More Individualized Instruction

We know that often students with disabilities as well as other low achievers will require more intensive, individualized instruction to master a specific skill or concept or learn positive behaviors. Research has shown that basic principles of effective education for these students should be explicit (they do not learn well only through discovery, and they often need to have a concept or large piece of information broken into smaller learning units), carefully monitored for growth, and presented in multiple ways (McDonnell, McLaughlin, & Morison, 1997; McLaughlin, Krezmien, & Zablocki, 2009). Students with more mild learning disabilities appear to benefit from good general education instruction with some additional time in small groups or individual instruction.

Sometimes the more individualized instruction can be effectively provided in a typical classroom through accommodations, technology, or other instructional arrangements such as using peer-assisted learning, using paraeducators, or having a special educator in the classroom. However, sometimes a student may need additional small-group or individual instruction for some period of time. Principals need to provide options for these services. For example, some schools have a resource room or support classes and centers that are available to students with and without disabilities. Students may receive academic assistance at the center on a regular basis or as needed.

What is important regarding such classes or centers is not necessarily the particular model used or which teachers or paraeducators staff them, but that they can be available to respond to individual student needs. The key point is for principals to be flexible in designing how staff might be used and to base decisions on careful assessment and analysis of student progress in meeting learning goals and standards and the types of supports he or she requires.

Resources for Identifying Effective Practices for Students With Disabilities

There are numerous organizations and websites designed to assist school personnel with the process of selecting appropriate, effective instructional practices for all students, including specific practices that are designed to target students with disabilities. A few organizations that focus on providing information on effective research-based practices are provided in the following list. Contact the special education administrator in your district for additional local and national organizations and websites. Also see appendix A (page 63) for additional special education resources, and visit **go.solution-tree .com/specialneeds** for links to the websites mentioned in this book.

- Council for Exceptional Children (www.cec.sped.org)

- National Autism Center (www.nationalautismcenter.org)

- National Center for Learning Disabilities (www.ncld.org)

- National Dissemination Center for Children With Disabilities: Evidence for Education (http://nichcy.org/research/ee)

- What Works Clearinghouse (http://ies.ed.gov/ncee/wwc)

Effective Classroom Strategies

There are a number of research-based strategies that a classroom teacher or school might adopt that have been proven to be effective with students with disabilities as well as struggling learners. Some of these practices, such as response to intervention and positive behavior supports, we discuss elsewhere in this book (see chapters 2 and 5, respectively). Effective principals not only understand the importance of using research-based strategies to enhance student learning but also seek ways to help teachers and specialized school personnel identify strategies that meet the learning needs of the students in their classroom and targeted learning goals in the curriculum. Principals can support their teachers and specialized school personnel by assigning manageable caseload responsibilities, identifying and offering professional development opportunities to develop collaborative teaching and learn new instructional strategies, and by providing teachers with shared work time to analyze results of progress-monitoring activities and identify new strategies for implementation (DiPaola & Walther-Thomas, 2003).

A great deal of research exists pertaining to strategies that are effective with students with disabilities. By *effective*, we mean that they have been shown to result in significant increases in achievement or improvements in social, emotional, and behavioral areas. Following is a summary of some of that research.

Peer-Assisted Learning Strategies (PALS)

Developed by Fuchs and Fuchs at Vanderbilt, PALS is one strategy that has been very effective with students with SLD and other low achievers in grades K–6 in providing more intensive and focused academic instruction. In PALS, students work in pairs or small groups to provide tutoring. For instance, in reading, students are taught three reading strategies: retelling (sequencing information), paragraph shrinking (generating main idea statements), and prediction relay (generating and evaluating predictions). In addition to being trained in each of the reading strategies, students are taught to correct their partner's reading errors, award points for correct responses, and provide consistent encouragement and feedback. Developers recommend that tutoring sessions last approximately thirty-five minutes and be conducted three to four times a week (Vanderbilt Kennedy Center for Research on Human Development, n.d.). Visit http://kc.vanderbilt.edu/pals to learn more about peer-assisted learning strategies.

Explicit or Direct Instruction

Explicit or direct instruction is a highly effective strategy for teaching students with disabilities and other low achievers both academic and social and behavioral skills. Explicit instruction focuses on breaking down curricular goals and objectives into discrete tasks and teaching students specific skills.

As Nancy Marchand-Martella (n.d.) explains, key components of explicit or direct instruction include:

> (a) careful content analysis that promotes generalization (teaching the "big ideas" of instruction); (b) clear communication (the "wording of instruction"

as well as how instruction is sequenced and examples are introduced); (c) clear instructional formats (specifies what teachers are to do/say and what responses students should produce); (d) sequencing of skills (prerequisites are taught before a strategy is taught; easy skills are taught before more difficult skills; strategies/information likely to be confused are separated; instances consistent with a rule are taught before exceptions); and (e) track organization (activity sequences are targeted that teach skills over multiple lessons to ensure firm responding).

Organization of instruction centers on (a) instructional grouping (using flexible skill grouping as compared to "tracking"); (b) instructional time (increasing academic learning time—the time students are engaged with high success rates); and (c) continuous assessment (providing ongoing in-program assessments to inform instructional practice).

According to Elaine Mulligan (2011), other strategies that have been shown to be promising or very effective include:

- **Mnemonic strategies**—Highly effective

- **Spatial organizers** [including graphic organizers]—Effective

- **Classroom learning strategies** (e.g., study skills instruction, note-taking strategies)—Very effective

- **Computer-assisted instruction** (CAI)—Moderately effective

- **Peer mediation**—Effective

- **Study aids** (e.g., study guides, text outlines)—Promising, but needs more study

- **Hands-on or activity-oriented learning**—Appears effective, but needs more study

As we stated in the introduction to this book, if principals are to be instructional leaders, it is important that they are informed about which strategies and practices are considered to be the most effective with students with disabilities as well as other low-achieving students. This knowledge can help principals determine the types of arrangements that might need to be made to support these students. The following is a list of tips on how principals can support effective, inclusive special education programs within their schools:

- **Provide leadership.** The principal plays a crucial role by actively involving and sharing responsibility with the entire school staff in planning and carrying out strategies that make the school successful (Lipsky & Gartner, 1997).

- **Create a community.** The inclusive school is a community in which all teachers share responsibility for all students. The teachers believe that every student can succeed and belongs in the mainstream of school and community life (Tomlinson, 2000).

- **Partner with parents.** Parents should be viewed as allies, not adversaries. They can be essential partners in the education of their children and can help make the school a true community (Lipsky & Gartner, 1997). Keeping parents informed about how their children will be educated and the supports the school will provide will aid in building a positive relationship.

- **Promote collaborative teaching and learning.** Teachers need to work together to design effective instructional strategies. Teachers can promote collaboration skills among students with and without disabilities through peer tutoring, buddy systems, and cooperative learning (Ferguson, 1997; Lipsky & Gartner, 1997). Principals can foster collaborative teaching by providing the time for teachers to work together and discuss how to differentiate instruction in the classroom and strategize about how to work with struggling learners.

- **Provide flexible school structures and learning environments.** Principals provide important logistical support for creating inclusive classes. This includes such things as ensuring that classroom rosters are balanced, scheduling team teacher work hours to promote collaboration, and ensuring adequate physical space or other arrangements needed for students with disabilities are made available (Lipsky & Gartner, 1997). In addition, principals are key in allowing teachers flexibility in how they choose to instruct students and providing scheduled time for weekly collaborative planning. Finally, to prevent teachers feeling overwhelmed, ensure that you do not overload any one class with too many students who require more instructional support, such as those with IEPs or other struggling learners.

- **Foster data-driven instruction and high standards.** Principals set the tone for the building when they expect every student to meet standards. Principals should ensure that every teacher understands how to monitor the progress of each student through the use of a variety of assessment tools. Specifically for students with disabilities in general education classrooms, it is important that the principal ensure that teachers review assessment data on a regular basis to make sure that the students are progressing.

- **Build a schoolwide behavior system.** The social and behavioral development of children needs to be supported in the school in order to foster a positive learning environment for all. By instituting a schoolwide and classwide behavior plan to help inclusive classrooms be less vulnerable to discipline and behavior problems, you can create an environment that promotes classroom friendships and cooperation and guards against bullying and teasing.

- **Provide multiple opportunities for professional development.** The principal must promote inclusive practices through joint professional development opportunities for general and special educators. Topics that may need to be addressed include assessment strategies, evidence-based practices for increasing learning in reading and language arts and mathematics, and social and behavioral development.

Teacher Professional Development

The move toward including students with disabilities in assessments and accountability systems has been stressful for many principals. It is understandable that principals will worry about the effects that the scores of students with disabilities may have on a school's performance. However, it is important that principals understand and provide leadership and support to teachers in how to use assessment data when making instructional decisions about students with disabilities by giving them opportunities to discuss ways to more closely align instruction for these students with the tests, and by encouraging them to individualize accommodations and to give students time to practice using them.

As emphasized throughout this chapter, providing high-quality instruction that supports the diverse needs of all students in the classroom is a process that requires teamwork among the principal, teachers, and specialized school personnel. Through fostering an environment that supports communication among all school members and a focus on identifying, implementing, and assessing the effectiveness of research-based strategies, principals can create schools that effectively meet the needs of all the students in their classrooms. In the next chapter, we will turn our focus to the discipline procedures mandated through IDEA, and schoolwide efforts that can reduce the frequency of discipline problems.

Discipline and Positive Behavior Interventions and Supports

Applying discipline policies to students with disabilities can be a confusing process for school leaders and is often misunderstood. However, protocols established in IDEA may help clarify the discipline process for principals. IDEA requires that certain procedures be followed in instances when a principal seeks to suspend or expel a student with a disability, and these procedures are based in the due process protections described in chapter 1 of this book. The following sections highlight important information principals need to be aware of in order to properly follow such procedures.

Questions Principals Ask

- What are the procedures for disciplining a student with disabilities?
- What is a manifestation determination, an FBA, and a BIP?
- How can discipline issues be avoided?

IDEA Discipline Procedures

The discipline procedures included in IDEA are part of the procedural safeguards of the law and are designed to protect the right of the student with a disability to receive a free appropriate public education and ensure the safety of the school environment. Under IDEA, students with disabilities are held accountable to the same disciplinary rules and procedures applicable to children without disabilities. A school may discipline a student with a disability in the same way and to the same extent as it may discipline a student without a disability for the same offense, subject to the following special provisions ("Placement and School Discipline," 2010):

- **No cessation of services.** This is the core of the discipline policies. Special education and related services may not be stopped for more than ten consecutive school days in any one school year. Schools may suspend a student with a disability for up to ten cumulative days in one academic year without having to offer any special education or related services to the suspended student with a disability. However, the special education and related services can be provided in settings outside the school, but the IEP team must meet to determine where the student should receive FAPE (the placement), and the parents must agree to the IEP decision to change the placement.

- **Stay-put provision.** IDEA requires that the student remain in his or her current educational placement pending administrative or judicial proceedings unless the IEP team and parents agree otherwise.

- **Manifestation determination.** If the school proposes to change a student's placement for more than ten days, the school must determine whether a student's behavior is a *manifestation* of his or her disability. Two questions must be answered: (1) Did the disability interfere with the student's ability to understand the impact and consequences of his or her behavior? and (2) Did the disability impair the student's ability to control his or her behavior?

- **No manifestation.** If the behavior is not a function or manifestation of the student's disability, the school has the right to discipline the student in the same way it would discipline a student without a disability. However, the school system is required to continue to provide the student with a disability the special education and related services identified in the student's IEP.

- **Manifestation of disability.** If the student's behavior is caused by or directly related to his or her disability, the school must take immediate action to address the behavior. The school is responsible for conducting a functional behavioral assessment (FBA) and developing a behavior intervention plan (BIP) to address the behavior. The student remains in or returns to the school unless the parents and school choose to change the educational placement through the IEP process.

- **Interim alternative educational settings.** The school may enforce a long-term removal for up to forty-five days in one academic year in an interim alternative setting, which can be residential, another school within the district, a school outside of the district, a police station, a library, and so on as long as the student continues to receive special education and related services as defined through the IEP. Repeated long-term suspensions are not permitted.

- **Exceptions for weapon, drug, and injury offenses.** If a student brings a weapon to school, uses illegal drugs in school, or causes serious injury to another person at the school, the principal has the authority to immediately remove the student and place him or her in an interim alternative educational setting for up to forty-five days. In this situation, a manifestation determination does not have to be conducted prior to placement in the new setting.

- **Unique circumstances.** When determining if a change of placement is appropriate for the student, the principal and IEP team have the authority to consider any unique circumstances on a case-by-case basis. Unique circumstances could include but are not limited to the student's area of disability, the functioning level of the child, and the intent of the behavior.

In addition to these provisions and procedures, principals will also need to be aware of student rights provided under additional laws when dealing with more severe disciplinary incidents.

Depending on the severity of a student's offense, at times, principals may have to involve law enforcement and must understand the proper procedures involved.

Reporting to Law Enforcement Agents or Juvenile Authorities

As Clark (1999) explains, "IDEA does not prohibit principals from reporting crimes to the police or to juvenile authorities" (p. 6). However, prior to reporting a crime committed by a student with a disability, principals should review the confidentiality requirements dictated by the Family Educational Rights and Privacy Act (FERPA). It is also important to know the district disciplinary procedures to ensure that you are adhering to district guidelines and requirements. Although FERPA generally requires that schools obtain consent from the parent prior to releasing a student's educational record, information can be released without parental consent to appropriate authorities when the safety or health of the student or other students in the school are in jeopardy. Visit http://www2.ed.gov/policy/gen/guid/fpco/ferpa/index.html for additional information about FERPA.

Zero-Tolerance Policies

The Gun-Free Schools Act of 1994 required every state to enact legislation that authorized public school officials to expel students who bring guns to school. With the impetus provided by the 1999 Columbine High School tragedy, many school districts adopted zero-tolerance policies that target weaponry and drugs in schools. Still, students with disabilities are protected by IDEA against expulsion under a zero-tolerance policy if the student's behavior is a manifestation of his or her disability. However, schools do have the right to obtain a court order for a removal or change in placement of a student who presents a serious danger to either him- or herself or others.

As of 2012, support for zero-tolerance policies is waning, and many school districts are implementing alternatives to zero-tolerance policies to address behavior problems. For example, school districts might implement a bullying prevention or threat assessment program. In general, these types of programs are implemented schoolwide as prevention programs, incorporate the values of positive behavior interventions and supports, and include levels of intervention that vary in intensity—from strategies that are targeted to all students to strategies that are intended for small groups of students who are struggling with specific behavior problems to strategies that assist individual students who have demonstrated disruptive or violent behavior.

Overall, the primary aim of the discipline provisions under IDEA is to create safe school environments while also protecting the rights of the student with a disability. Whereas the information provided so far in this chapter explains the authority of the principal and the school once a problem has arisen, IDEA advocates for a proactive approach to discipline through the use and implementation of functional behavioral assessments and behavior intervention plans.

Detailed information about conducting FBAs and creating positive BIPs is available on the Center for Effective Collaboration and Practice website (http://cecp.air.org).

Functional Behavioral Assessments

Functional behavioral assessments are used to isolate the relationship or link between events and a student's behavior. FBAs are useful in targeting cause and effect so that positive behavior interventions can be developed to address the problem behavior. Conducting an FBA requires careful observation and documentation of what preceded a student's problem behavior (the target behavior) as well as the natural consequences (what happens after the behavior). The process generally is conducted over several weeks and includes not only documenting and recording student behavior but also interviews with parents and teachers who work with the student. When gathering information, the teacher and other school personnel conducting the FBA should not only identify the situations that are triggering the problematic behavior but also the students' strengths so that these strengths can be utilized and built into the development of an appropriate intervention plan. The goal of the FBA is to evaluate how the student's disability impacts behavior and what accommodations or modifications can be put in place to reduce or eliminate the inappropriate behavior. The FBA is then used as the foundation for developing a behavior intervention plan.

Behavior Intervention Plans

The purpose of a behavior intervention plan is to be proactive and avoid events that lead to discipline problems. The BIP is a written plan that clearly describes what behaviors are expected of the student and the consequences of behaviors. The plan may be written by the classroom teacher, a special education teacher who provides supports and services to the student, or a school psychologist or behavioral specialist. Generally, the BIP will include ways to modify the environment to facilitate appropriate student behavior, provide supports and accommodations to help the student maintain good behaviors, and provide positive reinforcements. The BIP should also outline the disciplinary process to be followed and, if necessary, procedures for handling behavioral crises. A BIP is a legal document that school personnel are required to adhere to once the document has been approved by school personnel and the students' parents. Visit http://projectstay.com/pdf/BehaviorInterventionPlan.pdf to see examples of developed BIPs.

In addition to encouraging the use and implementation of FBAs and BIPs to address specific targeted behavior for individual students, IDEA recommends that principals foster a schoolwide vision of proactively addressing student behavior through the use of positive behavior interventions and supports.

Promoting Positive Behavior: Heading Off Problem Behaviors

IDEA's discipline procedures are reactions to problem behaviors. Of course, it is preferable for principals and school faculty to be proactive and preventive in their efforts to avoid problem behaviors in the first place. IDEA encourages schools to implement positive behavior supports for all students, and particularly for those students with disabilities whose behavior may result in removal from school. The goal is to teach students new behaviors and skills to deal with various school events and to avoid removal from school for behavioral code of conduct infractions. For students with disabilities, IEP teams can anticipate and manage behavior proactively by including in the IEP document functional learning goals that address the behavioral needs of the student. Prevention, intervention, and teaching replacement behaviors are the cornerstones of positive behavior support. Additional strategies to consider when establishing schoolwide discipline procedures are as follows:

- Create behavior systems that are simple, proactive, positive, and applied consistently.

- Develop rules and disciplinary procedures collaboratively among school staff, families, students, and community representatives to ensure that rules reflect the cultural values and educational goals of the community.

- Write clear, broad-based, and fair rules. They should include a code of conduct as well as specific rules, incentives, and consequences.

- Teach students their rights and responsibilities in schools, and post expectations of student behavior throughout the school.

- Provide supports to implement the rules.

- Evaluate the physical environment to ensure the school campus is safe and secure.

- Encourage cross-age tutoring that allows older students to help younger students who are experiencing difficulty.

- Develop interventions that help students learn positive ways of relating to others.

- Create a responsive interpersonal skills curriculum that focuses on enhancing interpersonal relationships, listening skills, setting goals, following directions, responding to peers, solving problems, managing and using anger in constructive ways, learning self-control, and accepting consequences related to inappropriate behaviors.

Visit the Technical Assistance Center on Positive Behavioral Interventions and Supports website at www.pbis.org for more information on strategies to encourage positive behavior.

The principal is key in preventing discipline problems among all students, including those with disabilities. The principal needs to be proactive and implement a schoolwide discipline program that emphasizes promoting desirable behaviors rather than punishing undesirable behaviors. The principal also must work with teachers, students, other school staff, and parents in developing schoolwide behavior expectations.

Three primary components of promising prevention programs include ("Prevention Strategies That Work," 1999):

1. Classroom prevention (positive behavior management, social skills instruction, and academic enrichment)

2. Schoolwide prevention (unified discipline approach, shared expectations for socially competent behavior, and academic enrichment)

3. School-family-community linkages (parent partnerships and community services)

Positive behavior interventions and supports is a proactive discipline model that focuses on preventing behavioral problems but also includes a process for intervening if inappropriate behavior problems arise. It is generally a schoolwide initiative that systematically teaches students in the school the behaviors that they are expected to exhibit while on school grounds. The model not only teaches expected behaviors but also provides reinforcement and recognition for students who model appropriate behaviors for students who are struggling with the behavior expectations. It is a three-tiered model of prevention strategies, including:

1. **Primary prevention.** Uses schoolwide and classwide strategies, including those that improve instruction and classroom climate. These strategies have clear expectations for behavior, have clear and consistent routines, encourage a positive and supportive climate, and provide role-modeling opportunities to practice positive behavior skills in different settings.

2. **Secondary prevention.** Uses interventions that are targeted on a small group of students, with the goal of reducing the number of students who demonstrate behavior that could become a serious problem or major violation of school code. Many of the students targeted at this level of support are also at risk for academic failure and may require additional academic supports.

3. **Tertiary prevention.** Uses interventions that are typically designed by a team of people, including behavioral specialists, to ensure that the needs of the individual student are addressed. This level of prevention is highly individualized. The goal of prevention at this level is to reduce the number, frequency, and severity of behavioral incidents among a small number of students with serious behavior and emotional difficulties. The students targeted at this level of prevention typically have IEPs.

An essential part of the PBIS process is collecting and using data on the behavior of the students in the classroom to make decisions about interventions, teaching strategies, and so on.

Want more information on discipline procedures and IDEA? The National Dissemination Center for Children With Disabilities has a host of resources in their Discipline, in Detail section of their website (http://nichcy.org/schoolage/placement/disc-details).

Discipline and setting behavioral expectations are important aspects of every school behavior plan. Principals with the tools for implementing proactive strategies such as PBIS and the development of FBAs and BIPs will find that they have fewer discipline cases to address. As discussed throughout this chapter, IDEA provides clear guidance on how a principal should proceed when faced with a student with a disability who has broken the discipline policies of the school. The next chapter will discuss the role of the parent in the education of the student with a disability and the parent's involvement in the school.

6

Encouraging Parental Involvement

An effective special education program is built collaboratively by school personnel and parents. The communication between the school and parents is a crucial component to enhancing the success of IEP development and implementation and achieving the intended goals of IDEA. With good communication between the school

Questions Principals Ask

- How do parents of students with disabilities commonly feel about schools?
- What are some strategies schools can use to build effective relationships with parents?

and home, parents are able to build on the strategies and interventions applied at school to foster improved progress in the student's annual goals, and teachers and other school personnel are able to learn more about the individual needs of the student through the insight of the parents. Creating this type of collaborative relationship between the school and parents of a student with a disability is a goal shared by parent advocates, administrators, and policymakers.

As the principal, you will need to set the tone for promoting and fostering effective and meaningful communication between the school and parents. As the leader of the school, it is crucial that you are able to involve parents of students with a disability in a positive way. Parents need open and regular access to the general education teacher, school counselors and psychologists, related service personnel, and the principal. Try to view the parents of students with disabilities as partners with the school as you work together to address the unique learning needs of the student, and encourage their active participation in helping you and your staff resolve issues that arise.

Working with parents of students with disabilities can be rewarding, but it can also be frustrating. Parents of a child with a disability experience many difficulties and challenges, particularly if the disability is severe. A child with a disability can have profound effects on the family as a whole, which can lead to a great deal of stress, anxiety, and frustration. Some parents are able to cope and to successfully adapt; others may not be able to. Sometimes parents have strong feelings of guilt and may blame themselves or each other for having a child with a disability, or they may blame physicians or other professionals, including teachers and administrators.

Further, parents may feel overwhelmed with the IEP evaluation and development process or frustrated with the school because they do not feel that the school understands or addresses the unique learning needs of their child. Effective communication will require that you are able to create an atmosphere in which the parents feel that their concerns are understood, their perspective is respected, and their knowledge about their child is valued. In other words, parents need to know that their voices are being heard and that the school respects the information that they have to share about their student.

Communications With Parents

Effective school-parent relationships are built on open, frequent interactions with teachers, the school counselor, psychologist, and principal. As the principal of the school, you will need to foster opportunities for parents to share their knowledge and their concerns about the child with a disability. It is through regular communication, open dialogue, and respect that a trusting relationship will form between the school and parents.

Unfortunately, it is not uncommon for parents of children with disabilities to become frustrated with school personnel when seeking services for their children. Parents of children with disabilities can feel isolated from the general education population, powerless, and unable to guide the education program of their student. They may feel that they have to continually fight for the services their child needs. Parents of students with disabilities also tend to be less satisfied with their child's education as contrasted to peers in general education (Newman, 2005). These feelings of frustration are only compounded when parents feel their only opportunity for discussing the educational program and progress of their child is during an IEP meeting. Further, parents often face a number of barriers in the IEP process itself, such as problems dealing with differing opinions; a lack of understanding about the school system, special education process, or technical language used; feelings of inferiority; and uncertainty about their child's disability (Lovitt & Cushing, 1999). As the leader of the school, you have the opportunity to reduce parent frustration by ensuring that parents are provided with information in a timely manner, included in their child's education on an ongoing basis, and valued as key members of the IEP team.

Effective Strategies to Promote Communication

The 1997 and 2004 IDEA amendments include several recommended strategies for working effectively with parents. For instance, when communicating with parents and encouraging their participation in their child's education, consider the following:

- Ensure that parents assist in identifying IEP goals. Parents should take part in IEP meetings and play an active role in setting goals.

- Ensure that parents know about and understand their rights, privileges, and due process.

- Inform parents of their child's progress and method of evaluation.

- Inform parents of major trends and issues in education.

- Ensure that parents know about other agencies that provide assistance.

To support these strategies and foster positive communication among schools and parents, IDEA has also funded and provided directions for the establishment of parent training and information centers in each state (for more information about these centers, see the lists of online resources in appendix A, beginning on page 63). Despite these efforts, many parents of students with disabilities continue to feel frustrated when communicating with the school, which perhaps suggests that some school personnel do not understand their legal obligations to parents of students with disabilities. Moreover, mere compliance with the law should never be the sole foundation of the school-parent partnership. A genuine school-parent relationship is premised on mutual respect and the desire to provide the best education possible for the student with a disability.

Ultimately, parents appreciate being informed—whether it is about the academic progress of their child or resources that can help them locate additional information. As the leader of your school, you are in the position to ensure the school staff are reaching out to parents to build a trusting partnership.

Conference Format for Effective Communication

Effective communication between school members and parents can be facilitated through the use of a planning tool that clearly and explicitly identifies the purpose or goals of the meeting, the problem that needs to be addressed, and recommended solutions. The following is a sample agenda that can be used to ensure that the meeting remains focused on goals, addresses the areas of concern, and maintains a positive and collaborative relationship among school staff and parents. It is recommended that you set a time limit for each section of the meeting in order to ensure that you address all steps during the time allotted.

1. **Identify a task headline.** Positively state the reason for the meeting. For example, "Today, we are here to identify some ways to support Johnny to reduce classroom outbursts."

2. **Analyze the problem.** At this point in the meeting, it is important to identify why this behavior is a problem or concern. Teachers can share information about strategies that have been tried that failed, and parents can provide information about whether or not the problem also occurs at home and, if so, what strategies have been successful in the home environment.

3. **Clarify specific goals.** Teachers and parents should then develop goal statements that specifically address the area of concern. For example, "I want to reduce the number of Johnny's classroom outbursts and support Johnny in redirecting his behavior if an outburst occurs."

4. **Brainstorm.** Parents and school staff share their knowledge and expertise to generate possible solutions to the problem.

5. **Select solutions, and make a plan.** Teachers and parents identify an agreed-upon solution and then work together to develop a plan with discrete tasks for implementation.

6. **Follow-up and ongoing support.** Prior to ending the meeting, discuss how teachers and parents will maintain communication about the implementation of the plan. Parents and teachers determine not only the frequency of communication but the methods as well (for example, email, telephone, or in-person meetings).

Source: Adapted from Bos, Nahmias, & Urban, 1999

Building Partnerships With Parents

IDEA clearly states that teachers, principals, and other school personnel must communicate with parents regarding the education and implemented programming for their children. Facilitating effective partnerships between the professionals in your school and the parents of children with disabilities will enable you to not only fulfill the rights of parents guaranteed under IDEA but also create a collaborative school atmosphere where parents and school staff alike feel respected and valued. Parent-professional partnerships allow parents and professionals an opportunity to work together and build on each other's knowledge and expertise to provide the best educational opportunity possible for the student. Schools that foster these types of partnerships are more likely to have high levels of trust among parents and professionals which leads to a school climate that is more positive and successful in solving problems related to teaching, learning, behavior, and educational programming.

As you work to create successful relationships among the teachers and parents in your school, consider the following principles of school-parent partnerships outlined by Turnbull, Turnbull, and Kyzar (n.d.):

1. **Communication.** Effective communication is fostered simply by: (1) being friendly, (2) listening, (3) being clear, (4) being honest, and (5) providing and coordinating information sharing. In terms of providing and coordinating information, families appreciate it when professionals provide information about current services, possible future services, the nature of their child's exceptionality, community resources, and their legal rights.

2. **Professional competence.** Demonstrate and share your commitment to providing high-quality education to the students in your school by setting high expectations not only for the students but also for the teachers.

3. **Respect.** Effective partnerships grow when partners treat each other with esteem and communicate that esteem through actions and words, honor cultural diversity, affirm strengths, and treat students and families with dignity.

4. **Commitment.** Fostering feelings of loyalty to each other by being available and accessible, going above and beyond, and being sensitive to emotional needs will help build an effective partnership.

5. **Equality.** Ensuring that each partner has roughly equal opportunity and talent to influence the decisions that the partners make will promote equality. Professionals who keep equality in their partnerships share power, foster empowerment, and provide options.

6. **Advocacy.** This principle relates to speaking out and taking action to pursue a cause on a personal, organizational, or societal level. To advocate effectively, professionals should seek win-win solutions, prevent problems, pinpoint and document problems, and form alliances.

7. **Trust.** This is the partnership principle that holds all of the other principles together. Without trust, the partnership is weak or may not even exist. Building trust means having confidence

in another person's word and judgment and believing that the trusted person will act in the best interest of the person who trusts him or her. It is based on being reliable, using sound judgment, maintaining confidentiality, and having confidence in your decisions.

School personnel often assume that parents who do not interact with them do not care about their child's education. However, since communication parents receive from schools is often negative, parents may assume that any communication from the school means their child is in trouble, making them less interested in initiating communication. Parents may feel alienated from schools for a variety of reasons. For example, a parent's own negative school experiences, such as dropping out of school or lacking confidence in school, may create stress for a parent needing to advocate for their student to receive services. Lack of parental participation can also result from career responsibilities that prevent parents from attending meetings during the day or inhibit their participation in after-school or evening schoolwide activities. Finally, schools should be sensitive to differences in cultural expectations of the school-parent relationship among parents of different ethnicities and supportive of parents who have limited fluency in English (Lovitt & Cushing, 1999).

The involvement of parents, whether those are parents of a student with a disability or parents of nondisabled students, can lead to a more successful and positive learning environment for the students in your school. There are many ways to encourage and support parental involvement in the school environment. Ways in which schools can promote more active parent involvement include:

- Scheduling and structuring parent interactions to minimize discomfort for them

- Clarifying for parents how they can help

- Encouraging them to be assertive

- Developing trust

- Building on home experiences

- Using parent expertise

As a final note, maintain a list of national and local organizations—including their websites—to share with parents who are looking for additional information or are in need of resources. There are numerous organizations dedicated to providing information about specific disabilities as well as organizations focused specifically on helping and working with parents. The following are some examples of organizations that could be useful resources to parents of students with disabilities:

- Family Center on Technology and Disability (www.fctd.info)

- Parent Technical Assistance Center Network (www.parentcenternetwork.org)

- education.com (www.education.com/topic/special-needs)

See appendix A (page 63) for other helpful special education resources you can share with parents, or visit **go.solution-tree.com/specialneeds** for links to the websites mentioned in this book.

This chapter emphasized the importance of involving parents in the education of their children and in the school community as a whole. Ensuring open and frequent communication will help to encourage this involvement. Referring parents to disability- and family-focused organizations is yet another way to promote a positive, learning, and collaborative relationship with the parents in your school.

CONCLUSION

Final Thoughts for School Leaders

While this *Essentials for Principals* resource was written to provide school leaders with information they need to develop and maintain an effective special education program, it also highlights the complexity of the issues surrounding special education.

Many of these issues are legal ones, focusing on the law and what it means for schools. Other issues are educational, asking what programs or approaches seem to hold promise for helping students with disabilities achieve the educational standards. Efforts to build always-important relationships between schools and the families they serve are even more critical when the children involved have special needs. Finally, schools must find ways to provide safe, nonthreatening environments for their students and staff. A school cannot successfully address all of these issues unless the principal and other key staff members are knowledgeable about both the law and effective instructional practice.

The best advice might be to review your current practices and then select only a few to study and improve. For example, ask yourselves what aspect of your special education program—development of IEPs, collaboration between general and special education, or discipline problems—currently seems most in need of attention. Focus on that, using this *Essentials for Principals* guide to help your school improve its practice.

As the school leader, you can provide the structure and support needed for these efforts. Supportive principals understand the importance of providing the time and encouragement needed by general and special education teachers who are engaged in developing new approaches to provide effective educational opportunities to all students. Your efforts and your knowledge are critical.

APPENDIX A

Online Resources

Online Resources

Visit **go.solution-tree.com/specialneeds** for links to the websites listed in this appendix.

Assessment, Accountability, Data, and Outcomes

Assessment and Accountability Comprehensive Center (AACC)

www.aacompcenter.org

The primary aim of the Assessment and Accountability Comprehensive Center is to assist states and districts in their understanding and use of assessment and accountability systems that benefit all students, including students with disabilities. The Center provides multiple resources on the development and implementation of data-driven systems that can be used to inform instruction and monitor student learning and progress in the curriculum.

Data Accountability Center (DAC)

www.ideadata.org/default.asp

The Data Accountability Center provides technical assistance to states to help build their capacity in meeting IDEA's requirements for data collection and reporting. The Center's website not only has online training modules on data collection and submission but also includes data about children and youth with disabilities served under Parts B and C of IDEA.

Early Childhood Outcomes (ECO) Center

www.fpg.unc.edu/~eco/index.cfm

The Early Childhood Outcomes (ECO) Center, funded by the Office of Special Education Programs (OSEP), is charged with providing states with assistance in implementing high-quality outcome measurement systems for early intervention and early childhood special education programs. The Center's work focuses on (1) developing an outcomes measurement framework for states to implement, (2) technical assistance to support the early childhood community, and (3) analysis of state-level child outcome and family indicator data to inform policies and programs. Up-to-date information and resources are provided through their website.

Behavior Interventions and Supports

Center for Effective Collaboration and Practice: Schools and Special Education

http://cecp.air.org/schools_special.asp

This website, which focuses on improving services for children and youth with emotional and behavioral problems, includes a variety of resources on addressing problem behaviors. Reports available for download range from instructional materials on how to conduct a functional assessment or create a behavior intervention plan to information on promising practices and preventing school failure. There is also detailed information on conducting functional behavioral assessments and developing behavior intervention plans.

Technical Assistance Center on Positive Behavioral Interventions and Supports

www.pbis.org

The Technical Assistance Center on Positive Behavioral Interventions and Supports (PBIS) is funded by OSEP and brings together eleven technical assistance units across the United States to increase the implementation of positive behavior management systems in schools. The Center's website provides tools, videos, presentations, publications, and training materials on PBIS and its implementation in the school. The Center has also created a resource search guide to facilitate easy retrieval of information specific to individual interests and needs. Districts and schools in need of technical assistance can use the Center's PBIS state coordinator network to locate regional and state coordinators for support on the development and implementation of PBIS.

Disability Organizations

Council for Exceptional Children (CEC)

www.cec.sped.org

The Council for Exceptional Children website includes a wealth of information on all aspects of special education, including policy reports, professional development information, and the latest news and issues affecting everyone involved in the education of students with disabilities or who are gifted. This site offers an RTI blog, a bookstore, and current information on evidence-based practice and instructional strategies.

IDEA Partnership

www.ideapartnership.org

The IDEA Partnership facilitates interaction and shared work across professional and family organizations around common interests. The website provides a wealth of information ranging from response to intervention, secondary transition, and users' guides on research-based instruction to topical issues on IDEA 2004 regulations and statutes. The partnership fosters communities of practice and dialogue to solve problems and improve learning for all students.

National Dissemination Center for Children With Disabilities (NICHCY)

http://nichcy.org

NICHCY is a central source of information on disabilities in infants, toddlers, children, and youth. The NICHCY website provides information ranging from the law, regulations, and specific implementation guidance to detailed information and resources for each of the disability types. The site also includes easy-to-read information on IDEA 2004, articles on a variety of educational topics, and lists of state resources to help connect professionals with the disability agencies and organizations in their states.

Dispute Resolution

National Center on Dispute Resolution in Special Education (CADRE)

www.directionservice.org/cadre

The primary mission of the National Center on Dispute Resolution in Special Education (CADRE) is to decrease the need for expensive due process hearings by improving state, district, and school capacities in resolving special education disputes. The Center has created a user-friendly continuum of processes and practices on responding to and resolving special education disputes that is fully searchable and defines the timelines and requirements for each step of the process. Additional resources on dispute resolution can be located in their searchable literature database. The Center's website also includes a section devoted to families which includes numerous downloadable resources designed to increase understanding of IDEA requirements.

Instruction, Strategies, and Interventions

Co-Teaching Connection

www.marilynfriend.com

This website provides resources for administrators and teachers on the implementation of effective co-teaching strategies. Lesson plans and resource documents are available.

Center on Instruction (COI)

www.centeroninstruction.org

The Center on Instruction, funded by the U.S. Department of Education, provides information on research-based interventions and instructional strategies to support high-quality instruction for all students. The website contains numerous free resources, including practitioner guides, professional development materials, examples from the field, and syntheses of recent research to assist states, districts, and local educators as they work to improve the learning outcomes for all students.

Intervention Central

www.interventioncentral.org

Intervention Central offers free tools and resources to help school and district staff and parents implement response to intervention strategies and promote positive classroom behaviors. The website includes both academic and behavioral research-based interventions and information on curriculum-based measurement, including manuals and forms to support implementation in the classroom and school. Intervention Central also provides a variety of customizable workshops to schools and districts on implementation of response to intervention.

What Works Clearinghouse (WWC)

http://ies.ed.gov/ncee/wwc

Established in 2002 by the U.S. Department of Education, the mission of the What Works Clearinghouse is to serve as a central source of research-based interventions and strategies proven to be effective in education. WWC uses a comprehensive review process for evaluating interventions, strategies, and tools prior to including them in the clearinghouse. WWC has created multiple ways for users to search the database and find information.

Parent Support

ALLIANCE National Parent Technical Assistance Center

www.parentcenternetwork.org/national/aboutus.html

The charge of the ALLIANCE National Parent Technical Assistance Center is to provide support to parent centers, parent training and information centers, and community parent resource centers throughout the United States. The Center provides technical assistance and develops fact sheets and a newsletter on key issues. Users can also access their regional parent technical assistance centers and local parent centers through the ALLIANCE National website.

education.com: Special Needs

www.education.com/topic/special-needs

Parents are the primary target audience of this website. Education.com is designed to empower parents by providing resources ranging from educational activities and project ideas to do at home to articles about challenges faced in parenthood. The website includes an open-ended question area for parents to solicit free expert advice as well as communicate with other parents. Education.com provides resources to support parents of both general education and special education students, and resources are searchable by topic, disability type, age, grade, or academic service.

Family Center on Technology and Disability (FCTD)

www.fctd.info

The primary focus of the Family Center on Technology and Disability is to provide information and resources about assistive technologies (AT) that can be used to support students with disabilities at home, in their communities, and in their schools. The FCTD website houses two searchable databases: a resource review database which includes hundreds of different types of AT devices and instructional technology resources, and a member organization database which allows users to search for organizations within their state or region that address their areas of interest. The Center also prepares and disseminates monthly newsletters on AT, hosts online discussions, provides fact sheets and family guides for download, and provides an AT glossary.

Policy and Legislation

Building the Legacy: IDEA 2004

http://idea.ed.gov

The purpose of the Building the Legacy: IDEA 2004 website is to increase capacity in understanding and interpreting IDEA's statutes and associated regulations. The website was developed by the Office of Special Education and Rehabilitative Services and the Office of Special Education Programs in the U.S. Department of Education and provides a wealth of information about key IDEA topics, provisions, and requirements. Examples of resources available include topic briefs, training materials, webcasts and presentations, and Q & A documents on each key topic in IDEA as well as IDEA's statutes and regulations.

Council of Educators for Students With Disabilities: Resources

www.504idea.org/Council_Of_Educators/Resources.html

This organization hosts conferences on Section 504 and key IDEA topics and offers customized professional development workshops that are designed to meet the unique needs of the school, district, or state. Written materials developed for conference presentations and customized workshops are available for download through the website.

National Dissemination Center for Children With Disabilities: IDEA—The Individuals With Disabilities Education Act

http://nichcy.org/laws/idea

NICHCY's charge is to nationally disseminate information about types of disabilities, programs and services for children and youth with disabilities, IDEA, and best practice research-based interventions and strategies. Included on the website is a section about IDEA which includes: (1) brief summaries of key IDEA topics, (2) the IDEA statutes and regulations, (3) guidance on IDEA from the U.S. Department of Education, and (4) training materials on the provisions and requirements of IDEA.

U.S. Department of Education

www.ed.gov

This website includes information about the law, IDEAs that Work, and recent research and resources on a variety of education topics, including those related to special education. Also see the Department of Education's web page at http://www2.ed.gov/policy/elsec/guid/states/index .html for information on No Child Left Behind legislation and policies.

U.S. Department of Education: Office of Special Education Programs (OSEP)

www.ed.gov/about/offices/list/osers/osep/index.html

The Office of Special Education Programs is the federal agency within the U.S. Department of Education responsible for implementation and oversight of the IDEA legislation and regulations within the states. OSEP funds grants and contracts involving model demonstration programs, teacher education, technical assistance, and dissemination of research-based information. A number of topical products for parents, teachers, and administrators are available on this website.

Qualified Personnel

Council for Exceptional Children: Professional Development

www.cec.sped.org/AM/Template.cfm?Section=Professional_Development

The professional development (PD) page on CEC's website provides information about the CEC Professional Development Services Team. This team of individuals is responsible for providing professional training workshops for teachers and administrators educating students with disabilities. Specialized workshops include life centered career education (LCCE) training and NCATE/CEC accreditation review preparation assistance. Workshops can also be customized to meet the unique needs of a school or district. In addition to PD workshops, CEC offers interactive webinars and the CEC Learning Center, which allows users to download sessions from the CEC annual convention.

Learning Forward

www.learningforward.org

Learning Forward is dedicated to enhancing professional development opportunities for educators to improve the learning outcomes of all students. Learning Forward has developed standards for professional learning which define the key characteristics essential to professional development to enhance teaching practice, build leadership, and impact student achievement. Learning Forward provides their membership with online activities such as webinars, e-communities, and a blog as well as a newsletter, annual conference, summer conference, and a two-and-a-half year intensive learning academy. The Learning Forward Center for Results provides intensive consulting services for individuals who are working to develop and implement new teacher effectiveness evaluation systems.

National Center to Improve the Recruitment and Retention of Qualified Personnel for Children With Disabilities (Personnel Improvement Center)

www.personnelcenter.org

The National Center to Improve the Recruitment and Retention of Qualified Personnel for Children With Disabilities (Personnel Improvement Center) was founded on October 1, 2008, under a new cooperative agreement between the National Association of State Directors of Special Education (NASDSE) and the U.S. Department of Education, Office of Special Education Programs (OSEP). The primary mission of the Center is to assist states in implementing effective systems for recruiting, preparing, and retaining highly qualified special educators, early intervention and related services personnel, and paraeducators.

National Dissemination Center for Children With Disabilities: What It Means to Be Highly Qualified

http://nichcy.org/schools-administrators/hqt?

This web page specifically addresses the requirements stated in NCLB and IDEA on being a highly qualified teacher. The web page provides a brief introduction to the requirements and compares the definitions stated in each of the two laws as well as some frequently asked questions and training materials on defining highly qualified personnel.

Regional Resource Center (RRC) Program

www.rrcprogram.org

The Regional Resource Center Program provides services to all states to improve academic outcomes for students with disabilities. Services provided through the RRC can include but are not limited to individual consultations, specially designed technical assistance, and training. There are six regional resource centers that work together and with other organizations to build a network of people committed to resolving similar challenges and issues.

Research Articles and Materials

Education Resources Information Center (ERIC)

www.eric.ed.gov

ERIC, sponsored by the U.S. Department of Education, Institute of Education Sciences, supplies users with bibliographic records of education journals and other published education materials, including full-text articles and documents as available. Content on this site is provided free of charge.

Response to Intervention

National Center on Response to Intervention (NCRTI)

www.rti4success.org

The National Center on Response to Intervention, funded by the U.S. Department of Education's Office of Special Education Programs (OSEP), assists states and districts as they work to learn about and implement RTI. This website provides a variety of resources on RTI, including charts, implementation tools, archived webinars, training modules, research syntheses, and short video clips of experts in the field addressing specific questions about RTI. The Center also conducts and publishes annual reviews of tools and interventions in progress monitoring, screening, and instructional programs.

RTI Action Network

www.rtinetwork.org

The RTI Action Network website assists school- and district-level personnel in implementation of response to intervention. The primary aim of the RTI Action Network is to facilitate and encourage the early identification of students at risk for academic failure and effective implementation of instructional interventions that address the needs of these students.

School Improvement

Equity Alliance at ASU

www.equityallianceatasu.org

The Equity Alliance at ASU helps districts and schools through technical assistance activities that foster the development of culturally responsive schools. Equity Alliance is committed to creating inclusive schools that value all students.

National Association of State Directors of Special Education (NASDSE)

www.nasdse.org

This website provides resources to assist general and special educators in continuously improving educational services and outcomes for students with disabilities. NASDSE provides free downloads and options to purchase print copies of important step-by-step implementation guidelines, resources, and tips for such important initiatives as response to intervention at the school level, the district level, and the state level. In addition to NASDSE's main website (www.nasdse.org), they sponsor the following: www.projectforum.org, www.ideapartnership.org, www.sharedwork .org, www.personnelcenter.org, and www.uscharterschools.org/specialedprimers.

Support for Secondary Schools

National Dropout Prevention Center for Students With Disabilities (NDPC-SD)

www.ndpc-sd.org

The National Dropout Prevention Center for Students With Disabilities provides technical assistance to states with a goal of creating sustainable programs that result in a reduction of the dropout rate and increase the likelihood of school completion among students with disabilities.

National High School Center

www.betterhighschools.org

The National High School Center is devoted to improving education programs at the secondary level. The website includes links to topical briefs, a blog on high school issues, archived webinars, and a free Microsoft Excel-based program (the Early Warning System) designed to help identify students who show early warning signs that they are at risk for dropping out of high school.

National Secondary Transition Technical Assistance Center (NSTTAC)

www.nsttac.org

The National Secondary Transition Technical Assistance Center assists states in their understanding of the transition provisions of IDEA. The Center provides technical assistance to states by identifying and disseminating information on successful evidence-based practices that enhance the postsecondary outcomes for students with disabilities.

APPENDIX B

Summary of Significant Changes in IDEA 2004

The following items describe important changes made to IDEA in 2004. The items are listed in the order in which they appear under the law.

1. **Eligibility determination.** Allows local education agencies (LEAs) to "use a process that determines if the child responds to scientific, research-based intervention" (National Research Center on Learning Disabilities [NRCLD], 2007) in the determination of learning disabilities. This can be used by LEAs instead of the ability-achievement discrepancy formula used previously. This change permits the use of response to intervention (RTI) in the eligibility process.

2. **Early intervening services.** Allows LEAs to use not more than 15 percent of their special education funds to provide "additional academic or behavior supports" (NRCLD, 2007) to at-risk students who do not qualify for special education services. There is a restriction: the funds must be used to deliver these supports within the general education environment.

3. **Short-term objectives.** Required only for students (generally less than 1 percent) who are taking alternate assessments aligned to alternate achievement standards.

4. **IEP progress reports.** Must include the "lack of expected progress toward the annual goals . . . and in the general education curriculum" but no longer must include the "extent to which . . . progress is sufficient to enable the child to achieve the goals by the end of the year" (National Association of State Directors of Special Education, Inc., 2006, pp. 125, 115).

5. **Transition.** Clarifies that the process begins at age sixteen, is more than a plan, and includes a coordinated set of services.

6. **IEP attendance and participation.** Given written permission from the parents of the student, IEP team members can be excused from a meeting if their area is not being discussed or if they provide a written report prior to the meeting. IDEA 2004 also provides for alternate means of participating in meetings.

7. **Pilot program for multiyear IEPs and paperwork reduction.** Provides up to fifteen states with authorization to pilot multiyear IEPs in which the IEP reviews coincide with triennial reevaluations as opposed to conducting a reevaluation of the IEP annually. States must apply to participate in the pilot program, which is voluntary.

8. **IEP team transition.** Addresses collaboration among service providers for children moving from early childhood (Part C) services into school-age (Part B) services.

9. **Transfers between school districts.** For in-state or out-of-state transfers, districts must provide comparable services to those described in an existing IEP until the existing IEP is adopted or a new IEP is developed, adopted, and implemented.

10. **Procedural safeguards notice/handbook on parents' rights.** No longer required to be distributed at annual review of IEP or at reevaluation. Must be distributed only once a year unless any of the following circumstances occur within the year: initial referral, parents request a copy, parents request an evaluation, or parents request a due process hearing.

11. **Statute of limitations.** Parents have two years within which to request a due process hearing regarding an IDEA violation.

12. **Due process complaint notice.** Parents who feel their child's educational rights are being compromised may file a complaint with the school district that is copied to the state. The school district must file a response within ten days or challenge the complaint's sufficiency within fifteen days. The state hearing officer has five more days to make a finding.

13. **Resolution session.** Mandatory before due process, the school district convenes a resolution meeting with parents and relevant members of the IEP team within fifteen days of receipt of the due process complaint. The school district has thirty days from the time the complaint is filed to satisfactorily resolve the complaint.

14. **Attorney's fees.** Parents' attorneys may be responsible for paying the school system's attorney's fees if the cause of action is determined frivolous, unreasonable, or without foundation. Parents may be responsible for the school system's attorney's fees if the cause of action was presented for any improper purpose, such as to harass, cause unnecessary delay, or cause increase in the cost of litigation.

15. **Qualifications for hearing officers.** The 2004 reauthorization includes qualification requirements for hearing officers, stating that hearing officers must have the knowledge and ability to interpret the intent of the statutes and regulations of IDEA as well as information about how previous court cases relate to the area of dispute. Hearing officers must be objective third-party individuals and, therefore, may not be involved with the student's education or care of the student in any way and cannot be employees of the state or local education agency. Finally, hearing officers must have knowledge of standard legal practice and the ability to make decisions about the problem and provide written resolution to the dispute.

16. **Stay-put provision.** Provision to remain in current educational placement pending appeal eliminated for students removed for more than ten days.

17. **Interim alternative educational setting (IAES).** Services received in an IAES must provide the child with programming and services necessary to enable him or her to receive a free appropriate public education, to continue to participate in the general education curriculum, and to progress toward meeting annual IEP goals.

18. **Manifestation determination review.** A behavior resulting in disciplinary action must be caused by or have a direct and substantial relationship to the disability to be determined to be a manifestation of the child's disability. The burden of proof, which was previously the responsibility of the school district, now falls on the parents to show that their child's behavior requiring disciplinary action was a result of the child's disability.

19. **Special circumstances.** Students may be removed to an interim alternative educational setting for up to forty-five school days for violations involving drugs, weapons, and serious bodily injury.

20. **Case-by-case determination.** School personnel can consider any unique circumstances on a case-by-case basis when determining whether to change the placement of a child with a disability who violates the school's code of conduct.

GLOSSARY

access to the general education curriculum. Ability of a student in receipt of special education to participate and progress in the general education curriculum, as ensured by the student's IEP team and document.

accommodation. A device, practice, or procedure that is provided to a student with a disability to ensure equitable access to the general education curriculum during instruction and assessments. The purpose of an accommodation is to reduce or even eliminate the effects of a student's disability. However, accommodations do not change the constructs being measured or taught and do not reduce learning expectations or performance standards.

alternate assessment. Assessment provided to students with disabilities who are unable to participate in regular assessments even with accommodations and for whom the state assessments do not reflect the curriculum of the child. The alternate assessment is appropriate for 1 percent or fewer of students who have been identified as having a disability. These assessments ensure states and school districts achieve educational accountability for all students.

assistive technology service. Support provided to a student to help select, acquire and use appropriate assistive technology devices.

behavior disorders. A term often used interchangeably in the field with the term *emotional disturbance*, which is used in IDEA. Some states and professionals have chosen to use the term *behavior disorders* as opposed to *emotional disturbance* because they believe it is a more accurate label of the students' disabilities and leads to more objective decision making.

behavior intervention plan (BIP). An individualized plan that targets inappropriate student behavior and is based on the data collected from a functional behavioral assessment. The BIP is designed to assist students with disabilities whose behavior is impacting the learning environment and their ability to progress in the general education curriculum. IDEA encourages the use of proactive behavior management strategies and supports, and the plan includes strategies that directly respond to the behaviors observed in the functional behavioral assessment.

behavior modification. The use of research-based strategies to improve behavior. After identifying the specific target behavior(s) to be changed, the professional systemically applies positive and negative reinforcement to reduce or extinguish the targeted behavior.

change of placement. Change in the setting in which the student receives educational services from that originally specified in his or her IEP. IDEA now includes a definition of what constitutes a change of placement in the disciplinary context. A disciplinary change of placement can occur if the student is removed from the current educational setting for more than ten consecutive school days or when the student demonstrates a specific behavioral pattern that results in removal from the current educational setting for more than ten days during the school year.

Child Find. A requirement under IDEA that ensures all states have policies and procedures to identify and evaluate children with disabilities (ages birth to twenty-one) and determine eligibility for special education services. Under this mandate, states are held accountable for each and every student in the state, and IDEA emphasizes the importance of designing policies and procedures that include identification and evaluation of children with disabilities who are homeless, living in migrant families, or are wards of the state.

co-teaching. A model of classroom instruction in which special and general education teachers share instructional responsibilities within the same classroom. The key feature is that both the general and the special education teacher have equal responsibility for planning and implementing instruction.

disproportionality. Refers to the over- or underrepresentation of a specific subgroup of students identified as needing special education and related services. States are required under IDEA to develop and implement policies and procedures to reduce misclassification and inappropriate placement of students by race and ethnicity.

due process hearing. A legal proceeding whereby the parent and the school district present information to support their viewpoint on a dispute and determine a solution. An impartial and trained hearing officer is assigned to the case and is responsible for listening to the information presented and determining the resolution to the problem (the hearing decision). States typically implement either a one-tier or two-tier due process system. In the one-tier system, the initial hearing is conducted through the state, and appeals are sent to court. In the two-tier system, the initial hearing is conducted by the school district, and any appeals are then directed to the state prior to going to court.

early intervention services. A system of coordinated services for students who do not receive special education services and supports but that are at risk for academic failure. Services are targeted on students in the early grades (K–3) but may apply for any student in grades K–12.

emotional disturbance. A disability category defined in IDEA as a condition whereby a student exhibits inappropriate behaviors, an inability to build or sustain peer relationships, anxiety, depression, or general difficulty in learning that cannot be explained through cognitive, sensory, or health factors. The student must exhibit these behaviors or characteristics over a long period of time and to such a degree that the student's educational performance is impacted. See Assistance to States for the Education of Children With Disabilities, 2010a, for the federal definition of emotional disturbance.

free appropriate public education (FAPE). A primary provision under IDEA that states that all children with disabilities must be provided with individualized instruction that meets the unique needs of the student, instruction must be provided at no cost to the parents, and the instruction must be aligned to state standards.

functional behavioral assessment (FBA). Process of searching for explanations, some of which may be connected to the classroom environment, for problem behavior. Using this information, a behavior intervention plan (BIP) may be developed as part of the IEP. Although not required for all students determined to be eligible for IDEA-related services, it is required if disciplinary problems trigger the need for change of placement decisions.

highly qualified special education teacher. A teacher who holds a bachelor's degree and full state certification and licensure, who can prove that he or she knows each subject in which he or she teaches, and who possesses knowledge in special education as well as subject areas in middle and high school. The IDEA definition is aligned with the NCLB requirements for highly qualified special education teachers. IDEA stipulates that if a teacher is working exclusively with students assessed using alternate achievement standards, they do not need to demonstrate knowledge in the subject areas of instruction.

independent educational evaluation (IEE). An evaluation of a student's academic or behavioral skills, which is conducted at the request of a student's parent by a person who is not employed by the public agency responsible for the education of the student. This evaluation must be provided in a timely manner and at no cost to the student's parents.

interim alternative educational setting (IAES). A change in placement triggered by disciplinary problems. An IAES is to be determined by the IEP team. The purpose of the IAES is to provide any student who is having behavior problems that impact his or her progress in meeting individualized educational goals with an educational environment and services that reduce and address the problem behaviors.

least restrictive environment (LRE). Setting in which a student with a disability is to be educated in accordance with the requirements of IDEA. Students with disabilities should be provided an individualized education program that facilitates progress in the general education curriculum in a setting with peers who are not disabled to the maximum extent appropriate.

manifestation determination review. An evaluation conducted by an IEP team to assess whether the problem behavior of the student with a disability was a manifestation of the child's disability.

mediation. Procedures established and implemented to allow disputes between schools or school districts and parents to be addressed through an alternative to more formal due process hearings. The procedures must:

- Be voluntary on the part of the parties, be provided at no cost to the parents, and be confidential

- Not be used to deny or delay a parent's right to due process

- Be conducted by a qualified and impartial mediator who is trained in effective mediation techniques (a list of qualified mediators can be obtained through the state)

If an agreement is reached between the school or school district and parents, the agreement must be documented, and this written mediation agreement is a legally binding document.

Some states and local education agencies require school districts to convene a meeting between parents who have refused mediation and a third party who is knowledgeable about the benefits of mediation to encourage parents to utilize the mediation option.

modification. A change in the curriculum or assignment that is intended to help the student learn and progress toward their individualized IEP goals. Changes are based on the student's learning needs and are therefore unique for each student. Typical changes include altering the reading level of material that the student is expected to learn or changing the assignment to make it easier.

related services. Supports and services provided to a student with a disability to facilitate progress in the general education curriculum. Services provided are dependent on the unique needs of the student. A few examples of related services include occupational and physical therapy, speech therapy, and assistive technology supports.

resolution meeting. Meeting to discuss a due process complaint filed by a parent. The school district must convene a resolution meeting within fifteen days of the complaint being filed. The purpose of this meeting is to attempt to resolve the problem in order to avoid a due process hearing. This meeting is required under IDEA and can only be canceled if the parents and the school district both agree to either waive the meeting or consent to entering into a process of mediation.

response to intervention (RTI). A process of evaluating students who are at risk of school failure, identifying targeted areas in which the student is struggling, and implementing research-based instructional interventions to address the areas of concern and improve academic success. Data are collected as interventions are tried to assess effectiveness. If a student does not respond to the initial intervention, another intervention of increased intensity is tried and student progress or lack of progress is recorded. Generally, there are three levels in an RTI model with the interventions increasing in intensity at each level. Students who move through all three levels of the RTI model and do not demonstrate an increase in their academic success are then referred for a special education evaluation. Data collected throughout the RTI process can be used as part of the evaluation data when determining eligibility to receive special education and related services.

special education. Individualized instruction that is designed to meet the unique needs of each student with a disability. This instruction must be provided to the student at no cost to the parent or family.

stay-put provision. Requirement that the student stay in the setting and receive the services specified in the IEP while any discussions or proceedings about a change of placement are pending—unless the state or local education agency and the parents agree to the change. However, if school personnel maintain that it is dangerous for the child to be in the current placement (placement prior to removal to the interim alternative educational setting) during due process proceedings, the local education agency may request an expedited hearing. The stay-put provision does not supersede IDEA components that permit a student to be moved from the setting specified in the IEP for ten days or less for disciplinary purposes.

supplementary aids and support services. Aids, services, and other supports IDEA requires schools and school districts provide to students with disabilities, in accordance with their IEP, to facilitate learning and progress in the general education classroom. Appropriate supplementary aids and services for a student with a disability must be defined in his or her IEP.

surrogate parent. A person appointed to ensure that the rights of a child are protected when no parent can be identified or located or when the child is either a ward of the state or homeless.

transition services. A coordinated set of results-oriented activities designed to improve the academic and functional achievement of the child with a disability. The purpose of these activities is to help the student as they move from the secondary school setting to postsecondary activities such as college, vocational education programs, work, or an independent living setting.

triennial assessment. An assessment conducted every three years after a child has been judged eligible for special education services to determine whether he or she is still eligible. Prior to the IDEA reauthorization in 1997, the regulation required the school district to repeat testing that had initially been done. In 1997, the law was changed regarding the requirements pertaining to eligibility evaluations. According to the 1997 IDEA amendments, evaluation data do not need to be collected on a student with a disability every three years to reestablish eligibility as long as the parent agrees that collection of these data is not necessary. These conditions for reevaluation were not changed in the 2004 IDEA amendments.

If the IEP team or parent believes that an eligibility evaluation would be beneficial to the student, the IEP team has the responsibility of reviewing extant evaluation data, assessing the student's present levels of performance, identifying and implementing appropriate evaluation assessments needed to determine if the student continues to be eligible for special education, and making a determination as to whether the student continues to be eligible for special education. The IEP team then identifies any modifications that would benefit the student.

REFERENCES AND RESOURCES

Ahearn, E. (2006). *Standards-based IEPs: Implementation in selected states.* Alexandria, VA: National Association of State Directors of Special Education. Accessed at www.projectforum.org/docs /Standards-BasedIEPs-ImplementationinSelectedStates.pdf on June 22, 2011.

Algozzine, R., Audette, B., Ellis, E., Marr, M. B., & White, R. (2000). Supporting teachers, principals—and students—through unified discipline. *Teaching Exceptional Children, 33*(2), 42–47.

Alternate assessments for students with disabilities. (2011). Accessed at www.cehd.umn.edu/nceo /topicareas/alternateassessments/altAssessTopic.htm on January 31, 2012.

Aspen's Administrative Development Group. (2000). *Reference guide to education law: School law yearbook.* Gaithersburg, MD: Author.

Assistance to States for the Education of Children With Disabilities, 34 C.F.R. Part 300 Appendix A (2002).

Assistance to States for the Education of Children With Disabilities, 34 C.F.R. § 300.344 (2006a).

Assistance to States for the Education of Children With Disabilities, 34 C.F.R. § 300.347 (2006b).

Assistance to States for the Education of Children With Disabilities, 34 C.F.R. § 300.114 (2009).

Assistance to States for the Education of Children With Disabilities, 34 C.F.R. § 300.8 (2010a).

Assistance to States for the Education of Children With Disabilities, 34 C.F.R. § 300.18 (2010b).

Assistance to States for the Education of Children With Disabilities, 34 C.F.R. §§ 300.305–311 (2010c).

Assistance to States for the Education of Children With Disabilities, 34 C.F.R.§ 300.323 (2010d).

Assistance to States for the Education of Children With Disabilities, 34 C.F.R. § 300.503 (2010e).

Assistance to States for the Education of Children With Disabilities, 34 C.F.R. § 300.508 (2010f).

Barnett, C., & Monda-Amaya, L. E. (1998). Principals' knowledge of and attitudes toward inclusion. *Remedial and Special Education, 19*(3), 181–192.

Bauer, A. M., & Shea, T. M. (1999). *Inclusion 101: How to teach all learners.* Baltimore: Brookes.

Bauwens, J., Hourcade, J. J., & Friend, M. (1989). Cooperative teaching: A model for general and special education integration. *Remedial and Special Education, 10*(2), 17–22.

Benz, M. R., Lindstrom, L., & Yovanoff, P. (2000). Improving graduation and employment outcomes of students with disabilities: Predictive factors and student perspectives. *Exceptional Children, 66,* 509–529.

Board of Educ. v. Rowley, 458 U.S. 176 (1982). Accessed at www.wrightslaw.com/law/caselaw/ussupct .rowley.htm on January 12, 2012.

Bos, C., Nahmias, M. L., & Urban, M. A. (1999). Targeting home-school collaboration for students with ADHD. *Teaching Exceptional Children, 31*(6), 4–11.

Brock, S. E. (1998). Helping the student with ADHD in the classroom: Strategies for teachers. *Communiqué, 26*(5), 18–20.

Burling, K. (2007). *NCLB regulations for modified achievement standards (2%): A white paper from Pearson Educational Measurement.* Accessed at www.pearsonassessments.com/NR/rdonlyres/680128F1 -B412-4A20-9A20-D4FD6AC613D6/0/wp0702.pdf on June 22, 2011.

Clark, S. G. (1999). The principal, discipline, and the IDEA. *National Association of Secondary School Principals Bulletin, 83*(610), 1–7.

Clark, S. G. (2000). The IEP process as a tool for collaboration. *Teaching Exceptional Children, 33*(2), 56–66.

Council for Exceptional Children. (2003). *What every special educator must know: Ethics, standards, and guidelines for special educators* (5th ed.). Reston, VA: Author.

Crockett, J. B., & Gillespie, D. N. (2007). Getting ready for RTI: A principal's guide to response to intervention. *Educational Research Service Spectrum, 25*(4), 1–9.

Dayton, J., & Arnau, L. M. (1999). *Special education law: A review and analysis.* Arlington, VA: Educational Research Service.

Deshler, D. D., & Schumaker, J. B. (1993). Strategy mastery by at-risk students: Not a simple matter. *Elementary School Journal, 94*(2), 153–167.

DiPaola, M., & Tschannen-Moran, M. (2003). The principalship at a crossroads: A study of the condition and concerns of principals. *National Association of Secondary School Principals Bulletin, 87*, 43–67.

DiPaola, M. F., Tschannen-Moran, M., & Walther-Thomas, C. (2004). School principals and special education: Creating the context for academic success. *Focus on Exceptional Children, 37*, 1–12.

DiPaola, M. F., & Walther-Thomas, C. S. (2003). *Principals and special education: The critical role of school leaders.* Gainesville: Center on Personnel Studies in Special Education, University of Florida.

Education Commission of the States. (2008). *ECS state policy database.* Accessed at www.ecs.org on September 20, 2011.

Etscheidt, S. K., & Bartlett, L. (1999). The IDEA amendments: A four-step approach for determining supplementary aids and services. *Exceptional Children, 65*(2), 163–174.

Evaluating children for disability. (2010). Accessed at http://nichcy.org/schoolage/evaluation on January 24, 2011.

Fast facts. (n.d.a). Accessed at http://nces.ed.gov/fastfacts/display.asp?id=64 on January 16, 2012.

Fast facts. (n.d.b). Accessed at http://nces.ed.gov/fastfacts/display.asp?id=59 on January 26, 2012.

Ferguson, D. L. (1997). *Changing tactics: Research on embedding inclusion reforms within general educa-tion restructuring efforts.* Paper presented at the meeting of the American Educational Research Association, Chicago, IL.

Fletcher, J. M., Coulter, W. A., Reschly, D. J., & Vaughn, S. (2004). Alternative approaches to the definition and identification of learning disabilities: Some questions and answers. *Annals of Dyslexia, 54*(2), 304–331.

Fuchs, D., & Fuchs, L. S. (2006). Introduction to response to intervention: What, why, and how valid is it? *Reading Research Quarterly, 41*(1), 93–99.

Fuchs, D., & Fuchs, L. S. (2009). Responsiveness to intervention: Multilevel assessment and instruction as early intervention and disability identification. *Reading Teacher, 63*(3), 250–253.

Fuchs, D., Mock, D., Morgan, P. L., & Young, C. L. (2003). Responsiveness-to-intervention: Definitions, evi-dence, and implications for the learning disabilities construct. *Learning Disabilities Research & Practice, 18*, 157–171.

Galis, S. A., & Turner, C. K. (1995). Inclusion in elementary schools: A survey and policy analysis. *Educational Policy Analysis Archives, 3*(15), 1–12.

Gersten, R., & Dimino, J. A. (2006). RTI (response to intervention): Rethinking special education for stu-dents with reading difficulties (yet again). *Reading Research Quarterly, 41*(1), 99–108.

Gersten, R., Keating, T., Yovanoff, P., & Harniss, M. K. (2001). Working in special education: Factors that enhance special educators' intent to stay. *Exceptional Children, 67*, 549–553.

Hang, Q., & Rabren, K. (2009). An examination of co-teaching perspectives and efficacy indicators. *Remedial and Special Education, 30*(5), 259–268.

Henry, S. (1999). Accommodating practices. *School Administrator, 56*(10), 32–38.

Hines, J. (2008). Making collaboration work in inclusive high school classrooms: Recommendations for principals. *Intervention in School and Clinic, 43*(5), 277–282.

Huefner, D. S. (2000). The risks and opportunities of the IEP requirements under IDEA '97. *Journal of Special Education, 33*(4), 195–204.

IDEA Partnership. (1999). *IDEA Part B final regulations: Regular education teachers as IEP members.* Alexandria, VA: National Association of State Directors of Special Education. Accessed at http://www2.ed.gov/policy/speced/leg/idea/brief3.html on January 6, 2012.

Individuals With Disabilities Education Act, 20 U.S.C. § 1400 (2004).

Johnstone, C. J., Altman, L., Thurlow, M. L., & Thompson, S. J. (2006). *A summary of research on the effects of test accommodations: 2002 through 2004 (Technical Report 45).* Minneapolis: University of Minnesota, National Center on Educational Outcomes. Accessed at http://education.umn.edu /nceo/OnlinePubs/Tech45/default.html on September 13, 2011.

Karger, J. (2004). *Post IDEA '97 case law and administrative decisions: Access to the general curriculum.* Wakefield, MA: National Center on Accessing the General Curriculum. Accessed at http://aim .cast.org/learn/historyarchive/backgroundpapers/post_idea97 on January 12, 2012.

Kaye, E. A. (Ed.). (2000). *Requirements for certification of teachers, counselors, librarians, administrators for elementary and secondary schools* (65th ed.). Chicago: University of Chicago Press.

Kronberg, R., & York-Barr, J. (1997). *Differentiated teaching and learning in heterogeneous classrooms: Strategies for meeting the needs of all students.* Minneapolis: University of Minnesota Institute on Community Integration. (ERIC Document Reproduction Service No. ED418538)

Küpper, L. (1999). *Questions often asked by parents about special education services: NICHCY briefing paper LG1* (4th ed.). Washington, DC: National Information Center for Children and Youth With Disabilities.

Küpper, L. (Ed.). (2000). *A guide to the individualized education program.* Washington, DC: Office of Special Education and Rehabilitation Services, U.S. Department of Education.

La Morte, M. W. (2005). *School law: Cases and concepts* (8th ed.). Boston: Allyn & Bacon.

Langerock, N. L. (2000). A passion for action research. *Teaching Exceptional Children, 33*(2), 26–34.

Lipsky, D. K., & Gartner, A. (1997). *Inclusion and school reform: Transforming America's classrooms.* Baltimore: Brookes.

Lo, Y., & Kretlow, A. G. (2008). *ERS focus on: What special education research tells us about teaching under-achieving students.* Alexandria, VA: Educational Research Service.

Lovitt, T. C., & Cushing, S. (1999). Parents of youth with disabilities: Their perceptions of school programs. *Remedial and Special Education, 20*(3), 134–142.

Marchand-Martella, N. (n.d.). *Direct instruction.* Accessed at www.specialconnections.ku.edu /?q=instruction/direct_instruction on November 10, 2011.

Marshall, C., & Patterson, J. A. (2002). Confounded policies: Implementing site-based management and special education policy reforms. *Educational Policy, 16*(3), 351–386.

McCoy, K. W. (Ed.). (1998). *Creating collaborative IEPs: A handbook.* Richmond: Virginia Institute for Developmental Disabilities, Virginia Commonwealth University.

McDonnell, L. M., McLaughlin, M. J., & Morison, P. (1997). *Reform for one and all: Standards-based reform and students with disabilities.* Washington, DC: National Academy of Sciences Press.

McLaughlin, M. J. (2009). *What every principal needs to know about special education* (2nd ed.). Thousand Oaks, CA: Corwin Press.

McLaughlin, M. J. (2010). Evolving interpretations of educational equity and students with disabilities. *Exceptional Children, 76*(3), 265–278.

McLaughlin, M. J., Krezmien, M., & Zablocki, M. (2009). Special education in the new millennium: Achieving educational equity for students with learning and behavior disabilities. In T. Scruggs & M. Mastropieri (Eds.), *Advances in learning and behavior disabilities* (pp. 1–32). Burlington, MA: Elsevier.

Mellard, D. F., & Johnson, E. (2008). *RTI: A practitioner's guide to implementing response to intervention.* Thousand Oaks, CA: Corwin Press.

Moody, S. W., Vaughn, S., Hughes, M. T., & Fischer, M. (2000). Reading instruction in the resource room: Set up for failure. *Exceptional Children, 66*(3), 305–316.

Mulligan, E. (2011). *What works: Effective teaching strategies for students with disabilities.* Accessed at http://nichcy.org/what-works-effective-teaching-strategies-for-students-with-disabilities on September 22, 2011.

Musgrove, M. (2011). *Memorandum: A response to intervention (RTI) process cannot be used to delay-deny an evaluation for eligibility under the Individuals With Disabilities Education Act (IDEA).* Washington, DC: U.S. Department of Education Office of Special Education and Rehabilitative Services. Accessed at www.rti4success.org/pdf/RTI%20Memo_1-21-11r.pdf on September 1, 2011.

National Archives and Records Administration. (2006). Part II: Department of Education: 34 CFR Parts 300 and 301. *Federal Register, 71*(156), 46549–46845. Accessed at http://idea.ed.gov/download/finalregulations.pdf on September 22, 2011.

National Association of State Directors of Special Education, Inc. (2006). *The Individuals With Disabilities Education Act: Comparison of IDEA regulations (August 3, 2006) to IDEA regulations (March 12, 1999).* Alexandria, VA: Author. Accessed at www.elc-pa.org/pubs/downloads/english/dis-IDEA%2097%20IDEA%2004%20side%20by%20side%20NASDSE.pdf on January 11, 2012.

National Center for Learning Disabilities. (n.d.). *Making the most of your parent-teacher conference.* New York: Author. Accessed at www.ncld.org/at-school/general-topics/parentschool-partnership/making-the-most-of-your-parent-teacher-conference on January 6, 2012.

National Center on Educational Outcomes. (2011). *Accommodations for students with disabilities.* Accessed at www.cehd.umn.edu/NCEO/TopicAreas/Accommodations/Accomtopic.htm on September 26, 2011.

National Research Center on Learning Disabilities. (2007). *How can early intervening services and responsiveness to intervention work together?* [Brochure]. Lawrence, KS: Author.

Newman, L. (2005). *Parents' satisfaction with their children's schooling: Facts from OSEP's national longitudinal studies.* Accessed at www.eric.ed.gov/PDFS/ED497545.pdf on January 6, 2012.

Nolet, V., & McLaughlin, M. J. (2005). *Accessing the general curriculum: Including students with disabilities in standards-based reform* (2nd ed.). Thousand Oaks, CA: Corwin Press.

Patterson, J. A., Marshall, C., & Bowling, D. C. (2000). Are principals prepared to manage special education dilemmas? *NASSP Bulletin, 84*(613), 9–20.

Placement and school discipline. (2010). Accessed at http://nichcy.org/schoolage/placement/disciplineplacements on January 25, 2012.

Prevention strategies that work: What administrators can do to promote positive student behavior. (1999). Accessed at http://cecp.air.org/preventionstrategies/prevent.pdf? on January 25, 2012.

Q and A: Questions and answers on highly qualified teachers serving children with disabilities. (2007). Accessed at http://idea.ed.gov/explore/view/p/,root,dynamic,QaCorner,2, on January 7, 2012.

Radius, M., & Lesniak, P. (1997). *Student success teams: Supporting teachers in general education.* Sacramento: California Department of Education.

Rieck, W. A., & Dugger Wadsworth, D. E. (2000). Inclusion: Administrative headache or opportunity? *NASSP Bulletin, 84*(618), 56–62.

Ripley, S. (1997). *Collaboration between general and special education teachers.* Washington, DC: U.S. Department of Education. (ERIC Document Reproduction Service No. ED409307)

Rosaen, C., & Lindquist, B. (1992). *Collaborative teaching and research: Asking "What does it mean?" Elementary Subjects Center Series (No. 73).* East Lansing: Center for the Learning and Teaching of Elementary Subjects, Institute for Research on Teaching, Michigan State University.

Seltzer, T. (1998). *A new IDEA: A parent's guide to the changes in special education law for children with disabilities.* Washington, DC: Bazelon Center for Mental Health Law. (ERIC Document Reproduction Service No. ED417535)

Slavin, R. E. (1996). Neverstreaming: Preventing learning disabilities. *Educational Leadership, 53*(5), 4–7.

Slavin, R. E., Kalweit, N. L., & Madden, N. A. (1989). *Effective programs for students at risk.* Needham Heights, MA: Allyn & Bacon.

Speece, D. L., & Hines, S. J. (2008). Identifying children who require different instruction in a response to instruction framework. *Perspectives on Language Learning and Education, 15,* 34–40.

Stevens, R. J., & Slavin, R. E. (1995). The cooperative elementary school: Effects on students' achievement, attitudes, and social relations. *American Educational Research Journal, 32*(2), 321–351.

Sturomski, N. (1997). Teaching students with learning disabilities to use learning strategies. *NICHCY News Digest, 25.* Accessed at www.nichcy.org/wp-content/uploads/docs/nd25.pdf on January 6, 2012.

Swanson, H. L. (1999). *Intervention research for students with learning disabilities: A meta-analysis of treatment outcomes.* Paper presented at Keys to Successful Learning: A National Summit on Research in Learning Disabilities, Washington, DC.

Thurlow, M. L., & Johnson, D. R. (2000). High-stakes testing of students with disabilities. *Journal of Teacher Education, 51*(4), 305–314.

Tomlinson, C. A. (1999). *The differentiated classroom: Responding to the needs of all learners.* Washington, DC: Association for Supervision and Curriculum Development.

Tomlinson, C. A. (2000). Differentiated instruction: Can it work? *Education Digest, 65*(5), 25–31.

Turnbull, A. P., Turnbull, H. R., & Kyzar, K. (n.d.). *Family-professional partnerships as catalysts for successful inclusion: A United States of America perspective.* Accessed at www.revistaeducacion.mec.es/re349/re349_04ing.pdf on January 20, 2012.

U.S. Department of Education. (n.d.). *Topic: Early intervening services.* Accessed at http://idea.ed.gov/explore/view/p/%2Croot%2Cdynamic%2CTopicalBrief%2C8%2C on June 22, 2011.

U.S. Department of Education. (1996). *Archived information: Report on the Section 504 self-evaluation—May 1996—Section 105.3*. Accessed at http://www2.ed.gov/pubs/Sec504/append-a.html#3 on January 9, 2012.

U.S. Department of Education. (2005). *Alternate achievement standards for students with the most significant cognitive disabilities: Non-regulatory guidance*. Washington, DC: Author. Accessed at www.ed.gov/policy/elsec/guid/altguidance.doc on January 2, 2012.

U.S. Department of Education Office for Civil Rights. (1998). *Student placement in elementary and secondary schools and Section 504 and Title II of the Americans With Disabilities Act* (Revised). Washington, DC: Author. (ERIC Document Reproduction Service No. ED426518)

U.S. Department of Education Office of Special Education and Rehabilitative Services. (2007). *29th annual report to Congress on the implementation of the Individuals With Disabilities Education Act*. Washington, DC: Author.

U.S. Office of Special Education Programs. (2000). *Schoolwide approaches to behavior*. Washington, DC: U.S. Department of Education.

Vanderbilt Kennedy Center for Research on Human Development. (n.d.). *Peer-assisted learning strategies: Strategies for successful learning*. Accessed at http://kc.vanderbilt.edu/pals on December 12, 2011.

VanDerHeyden, A. (n.d.). *Approaches to RTI*. Accessed at www.rtinetwork.org/learn/what/approachesrti on January 9, 2012.

Van Dyke, R., Stallings, M. A., & Colley, K. (1995). How to build an inclusive school community: A success story. *Phi Delta Kappan, 76*(6), 475–480.

Vasa, S., & Steckelberg, A. (1997). Paraeducators in school settings: Administrative issues. In A. L. Pickett & K. Gerlach (Eds.), *Supervising paraeducators in school settings: A team approach* (pp. 235–262). Austin, TX: Pro-Ed.

Vaughn, S., & Fuchs, L. S. (2003). Redefining learning disabilities as inadequate response to instruction: The promise and potential problems. *Learning Disabilities Research & Practice, 18*(3), 137–146.

Vaughn, S., Moody, A. W., & Schumm, J. S. (1998). Broken promises: Reading instruction in the resource room. *Exceptional Children, 64*(2), 211–225.

Vohs, J. R., & Landau, J. K. (1999). *PEER information brief: Improving the education of students with disabilities in an era of educational reform*. Accessed at www.fcsn.org/peer/ess/ideaib.html on September 22, 2011.

Wakeman, S. Y., Browder, D. M., Flowers, C., & Ahlgrim-Delzell, L. (2006). Principals' knowledge of fundamental and current issues in special education. *NASSP Bulletin, 90*(2), 153–174.

Walther-Thomas, C., Bryant, M., & Land, S. (1996). Planning for effective co-teaching: The key to successful inclusion. *Remedial and Special Education, 17*(4), 255–265.

Walther-Thomas, C. S., Korinek, L., McLaughlin, V. L., Williams, B., Fitz-Randolph, H., & Wood, S. (2000). *Collaboration for inclusive education: Creating successful programs (Instructor's Manual)*. Boston: Allyn & Bacon.

Wang, M. C. (1997). *Serving students with special needs through inclusive education approaches* (Report No. L97-11). Philadelphia: National Research Center on Education in the Inner Cities. (ERIC Document Reproduction Service No. ED419076)

Whelan, R. J. (1996). Classroom management. In E. L. Meyen, G. A. Vergason, & R. J. Whelan (Eds.), *Strategies for teaching exceptional children in inclusive settings* (pp. 303–310). Denver: Love.

Whitaker, S. D. (2000). Mentoring beginning special education teachers and the relationship to attrition. *Exceptional Children, 66,* 546–566.

Whitbread, K. (n.d.). *What does the research say about inclusion?* Accessed at www.wrightslaw.com/info /lre.incls.rsrch.whitbread.htm on September 13, 2011.

Yatvin, J. (1995). Flawed assumptions. *Phi Delta Kappan, 76*(6), 482–485.

Yell, M. L. (2006). *The law and special education* (2nd ed.). Upper Saddle River, NJ: Merrill/Prentice Hall.

Yell, M. L., & Drasgow, E. (2005). *No Child Left Behind Act: A guide for professionals.* Upper Saddle River, NJ: Merrill/Prentice Hall.

Yell, M. L., & Shriner, J. G. (1997). The IDEA amendments of 1997: Implications for special and general education teachers, administrators, and teacher trainers. *Focus on Exceptional Children, 30*(1), 1–19.

Zirkel, P. A. (1999). Zero tolerance expulsions. *NASSP Bulletin, 83*(610), 101–105.

INDEX

Critical Conversations in Co-Teaching
A Problem-Solving Approach
Carrie Chapman and Cate Hart Hyatt

In this practitioner's guide to building quality collaborative relationships, the authors explain co-teaching models and how co-teaching fits within school-improvement initiatives. Through practical examples and real-life stories, they present the critical conversations framework designed to foster dramatic improvements in the way co-teachers communicate.
BKF428

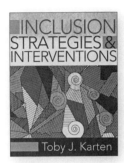

Inclusion Strategies and Interventions
Toby J. Karten

In inclusive classrooms, students with special educational needs are treated as integral members of the general education environment. Gain strategies to offer the academic, social, emotional, and behavioral benefits that allow all students to achieve their highest potential.
BKF381

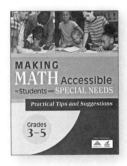

Making Math Accessible to Students With Special Needs (Grades 3–5)
r4 Educated Solutions

This manual offers tools and guidance to increase confidence and competence so that 99 percent of students will be able to access enrolled grade-level mathematics. Chapters cover federal and state legislation, research-based instructional best practices, and alternative instruction and assessment practices.
BKF289

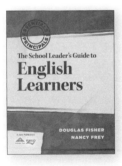

The School Leader's Guide to English Learners
Douglas Fisher and Nancy Frey

English learners face a difficult challenge: learning English *in* English. How, then, do you set reasonable expectations for developing proficiency? School leaders will learn how to assess the individual needs of ELs, how to create a quality instructional program, and how to evaluate performance.
BKF540

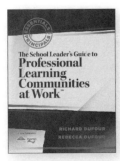

The School Leader's Guide to Professional Learning Communities at Work™
Richard DuFour and Rebecca DuFour

Are you a K–8 principal looking to implement the PLC at Work™ process? Explore the components needed to lay the foundation, including how to develop a structure that supports collaborative teams, how to focus on effective monitoring strategies, and more.
BKF489

Solution Tree

Solution Tree's mission is to advance the work of our authors. By working with the best researchers and educators worldwide, we strive to be the premier provider of innovative publishing, in-demand events, and inspired professional development designed to transform education to ensure that all students learn.

The mission of the National Association of Elementary School Principals is to lead in the advocacy and support for elementary and middle level principals and other education leaders in their commitment for all children.